Thinking about Thinking

Also by Stephen Lockyer

Education

The Christmas Survival Toolkit for Teachers
Money for Old Rope
100 Ideas for Primary Teachers: Outstanding Teaching
Hands Up: Questions to ignite thinking in the classroom
Acting Up & Writing Down

Fiction

Islandsphere
Bad Influence

General

Dadvice: Tips and techniques for fathers

Thinking about Thinking

Learning Habits Explored

Stephen Lockyer

teacherly

This edition published in 2015

Copyright © Stephen Lockyer

A *Teacherly* Publication

ISBN: 1518617913

Dedication:
I owe a huge debt of gratitude to the students I have taught for their willingness to be the petri dish of my ideas, many of which appear in these pages. I'd also like to dedicate this book to my friend Jane Ovenden, who religiously reads everything I write.

I have tried where possible to indicate provenance of any ideas which aren't mine, but if you are able to help identify these for future editions, please do let me know.   SL

Thoughts/ ideas/ issues? **Mr.lockyer@gmail.com** or @mrlockyer on Twitter.

"Thinking is the hardest work there is, which is the probable reason so few engage in it."

Henry Ford

Contents

VISUAL THINKING

STUDY THINKING

SELF-THINKING

How to use this book

Every book wants to be read, but some books prefer different ways to be read. Fiction likes the conventional start-to-finish approach, whereas this might not work for you, or for this type of book.

As a result, I have employed several strategies which are outlined to make this a more worthwhile read. Here are some hints and tips to help you make the most of this book.

Parts and Sections

Rather than using long chapters, the material has been divided up into Parts (themes) and sections. Sections are normally two or three pages long, making them quick to read and easy to absorb. They are also ideal for sharing as part of a staff meeting, mentoring session or support network. I have used bold font sizes for the title and subtitles to make each section easy to scan through and locate information too. While you are welcome to read this book backwards if you so wish, I would encourage you to read it in 'Part' blocks. These are clearly marked in the Contents.

Wide margins

These are for Cue Questions, part of the Cornell Notetaking Strategy, which can be found on page 143. If you are desperate to get going straight away, simply read each paragraph and write a question in the margin whose answer is the paragraph you have just read.

Footnotes

I decided to use footnotes rather than endnotes (all the references in the back of the book or chapter) for two key reasons. Firstly, I would encourage you to read further as you read this book. Many of the links to research papers are available as free .pdfs when you search for them online. Download them to read later. Secondly, I always feel slightly robbed when I read an academic or factual book and it finishes three quarters of the way through (I'm looking at you, *Superfreakonomics*) with the rest of the book filled with end-notes. It's like having your meal taken away three quarters of the way through eating.

Foreword: A caveat

This book will *not* make your students brighter, achieve more, or make you a better teacher. Reading this book won't change your life; in fact, simply reading it will take away some hours which could perhaps be better spent with friends or family.

However, if you try some of these strategies out, even in your own life, you will find that these small changes add up to something.

The difficulty with metacognition is that it is like a slow puncture - very hard to detect the change at first.

So please don't expect instant transformation of thinking from your students when you start using these ideas and strategies with them. Play the long game. Invest precious curriculum time in teaching the children not only thinking strategies, but stretch them by getting them to talk about their thinking. Challenge them to compare and contrast, justify their viewpoints, make sense out of things which they might otherwise complete automatically.

Have your students consider the way they learn, and how they can become independently better.

It's a fun ride, grounded in robust research, and if carried out thoughtfully and with care, will genuinely transform the way they approach learning, thinking and independent study, for life[1].

---

[1] It's a bold claim, but I'm unlikely to be around by the time you can realistically contest that statement.

I would love to hear of teachers and schools who adopt some of he strategies and approaches outlined in this book, especially if they are willing to allow me to share their stories in future editions.

With a text using such a wide range of sources, both academic and anecdotal, there are bound to be small errors made, so clarifications and adjustments are also welcomed. Please do make contact with me using the details at the start of this book.

I am aware that I began this book wanting to find answers to the questions I had about metacognition. I am also aware that it is perhaps too large a topic to cover in one single book, or that I haven't covered all the areas of interest that all the readers may have. If you have ideas for sub-topics which you'd like me to explore in further editions, I'd like to hear from you too!

Stephen Lockyer
October, 2015

INTRODUCTION

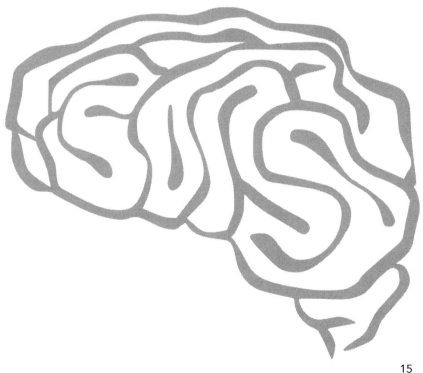

1. Speed Awareness (of) Course

We process so many things at lightning speed that our brain cannot help but prioritise, filter and omit information, which at some points may be key; even life-changing.

The trouble is, a vast amount of this is done without or knowledge or explicit permission. So how do we know when to take our brains off automatic pilot?

With experience behind the wheel of a car and a legally-necessary dial in front of them, how and why do drivers exceed the limit so often? It is the multitude of processes and inputs needed to drive that remove this fundamental aspect of driving.

In some counties of England and Wales, speeding motorists can receive either points on their driving licence for exceeding the limit, or pay to attend a Speed Awareness course. These have grown in popularity, and have been shown to vastly reduce speeding in the future[2]. Indeed, a fringe benefit is that those attending are likely to share tips learned with friends and family members.

As a family member of someone who attended a course, I was someone who gained this benefit with the use of one small tip given to attendees on their training.

---

[2] "Research reveals value of speed awareness courses." 2013. 23 Jul. 2015 <http://www.roadsafetygb.org.uk/news/2629.html>

It is incredibly simple, yet I've used it time and time again. Here it is:

When driving late at night and you are feeling distracted, narrate your journey aloud to yourself, saying everything you are seeing and doing.

I often find myself in this position, and it really has made a discernible difference. Making something which is normally subconscious become explicit forces you to acknowledge your surroundings in a way you wouldn't normally do - and it also heightens your awareness. Too often I have arrived at a location with only the vaguest recollection of my actual journey there. By narrating my experience, it creates a connection to what I am doing in a way which doesn't regularly happen.

Reflecting on this, how much else aside from driving do we carry out without actually thinking? More importantly, what are we missing? If something as vital as being aware of our road sense in a car is unreliable, what impact does this have on something as important as being witness to a crime[3] or or even our memories themselves?[4]

---

[3] "Eyewitness testimony " <https://en.wikipedia.org/wiki/Eyewitness_testimony>

[4] "False memory " <https://en.wikipedia.org/wiki/False_memory>

Most crucially for us as Educators though is the impact (or not) of allowing automatic pilot to occur in our classrooms, in our teaching, and in our students' learning. This is where our tacit state steps in and takes over.

Given the number of pupils we have to teach, the hours spent in front of the classroom, and the huge number of decisions made based on tens of thousands of variables, is this such a bad thing after all? Wouldn't we stop functioning if we gave careful thought about each decision, rather than using our gut teacher instinct to process and implement change?

In other words, is automatic pilot teaching such a bad thing?

2. The joy of tacit

I accept that this is one of my favourite words - but how can understanding what this word means, and what effect it can have on your teaching, is one of the keys to successful teaching. It also explains how an experienced teacher can 'take the temperature' of a classroom in seconds - sometimes before even entering the room.

The dictionary definition of tacit explains it simply: *"understood or implied without being stated."* So what does this mean in a classroom setting?

In short, it means that your brain is able to process an array of different variables without having to actively go through a mental checklist in your head, in the way an NQT (Newly Qualified Teacher) might have to at the start of their career, and understandably so, given the nature of the profession.

However, the pedagogy of teaching, that Art that you build in your formative years, can make much thinking practice tacit. Consider a senior member of staff coming to you at the start of the day, a scribbled piece of paper in their hands and wearing a furrowed brow...

"I'm afraid I'm going to have to ask you to cover 6S in Geography this afternoon. They've been looking at contrasts between town and country environments. There is some work set I think…"

Putting aside the frustration of losing some non-contact time you'd been looking forward to, already your brain is processing this information subconsciously. 6S are the tricky class with a few 'characters' you've come across before. It's in the afternoon, which means a different outlook and attention span to 9.15am. Work set? Doubtful, given that teacher. What could you draw on to show the contrast they've been exploring?

In those first few seconds, whether you are aware of it or not, your tacit knowledge of the class, the students, the time of day (and day itself; indeed the point in the term) and your own subject knowledge have all scanned through your mind. You might actually be excited by this lesson. You could of course be dreading it.

Tacit knowledge of teaching is the life-blood of experienced practitioners. It is this knowledge which stops some from panicking, and encourages others to do so. It helps you to prepare by 'thinking for you' when you don't have the time or capacity to do this properly yourself. More than this, it was a factor even before you knew about it; the senior teacher who quickly devised the cover went through the same implicit process when deciding the cover itself. Would your knowledge and experience allow you to even be able to take this lesson? Tacit knowledge of ourselves, our students and our peers enables schools to carry on without grinding to a halt at every decision which is made.

Despite all this, tacit knowledge can also inhibit growth, produce prejudices and stereotypes which are necessary but hard to shift, and in essence, do the thinking for us, when often we need to switch to manual thinking in order to bring out the best in ourselves and our students.

But how can stereotypes help or hinder us, and why are they necessary?

3. Stereotypes and the mirror

It would be impossible to build a framework of every single person, item or experience presented to us. In order to manage all this input of data, our brain automatically recalls information using prior knowledge, experience and indeed prejudices and biases.

Much of the time this is a sensible approach for the brain to take. When speaking to a frail elderly person for example, we almost always speak slower and louder for them; our prior experience tells us that (so far) the majority of elderly people we have met in our life tend to have poor hearing. We adjust accordingly. We've all been caught out by this though; occasionally we meet an octogenarian with better hearing than ourselves, and with some (justified) relish, they inform us that "they aren't deaf you know."

So far, so understandable. We also all know about the dangers of putting labels on groups of students based on other opinions of them, or prior experience of that 'type' of student[5]. It often leads to lower expectations for 'low ability' students, and opponents of ability grouping say that while their diet is more specific, it encourages a widening of the achievement gap.

---

[5] "NEA - Research Spotlight on Academic Ability Grouping." <http://www.nea.org/tools/16899.htm>

Stereotyping and grouping informs our tacit response to them when teaching the students. In order to tackle this, we often need a tangible response which convinces us otherwise, and this needs to be either large or repeated enough for our in-built prejudices to be challenged. One well-hearing pensioner often isn't a large enough nudge to tip the balance. It would need a succession of sharp-eared elderly people in our lives to make this adjustment.

This also implies that we are right until we are proven wrong. How often do we actively challenge and realign our stereotypes and prejudices in school? Are we more likely to wait for the evidence to present itself, happy to let our tacit knowledge carry us along? What biases do we have, and are we even aware of them? In short, how often do we put a mirror to our own biases, whatever they may be?

4. Types of bias

We all succumb to bias in one way or another, and many times this can ground us in ways that make us feel comfortable and secure. Within each bias however is the danger that whomever our bias goes against can be misrepresented, misaligned or in the worst cases, treated unfairly.

These biases can be seen in our schools every day; like most aspects of human frailty, they are often easier to spot in others than ourselves. How many do you recognise in your School?

Status Quo Bias

Known as keeping things as they should be or have always been, at best this provides familiarity, at worst, complacency against any form of change. Where any change is seen as a loss, the emotive state of status quo bias can affect decision-making on a grand scale.

Any teacher who has suggested some new initiative in a new setting to a response of, *"but we've always done it this way"* is experiencing this bias. Does this sound familiar?

This is different to status quo ante, where there is a perception of superiority over a commonly-held viewpoint over a new systemic change. In Education this can pervade even the selection of reading material for a class[6].

Confirmation Bias

This is the tendency to favour, recall or interpret information in a manner which confirms our own beliefs. This can become more extreme and entrenched if someone is defending their opinion, even when greeted with the same information as another party. That troublesome lower group are being taught again, and when one student calls out, it can psychologically reinforce the opinion one might have of that group, rather than factoring in a multitude of environmental issues which might have caused this behaviour. Confirmation bias is pervasive in schools, and its impact cannot be underestimated.

The biggest danger with confirmation bias is seeking out information which proves an in-built hypothesis, ignoring any evidence to the contrary. I am guilty of this, having in the past set up hypotheses about people and letting them (unintentionally) lose against my game rules. I also recognise that with these rules, I was also setting people up to fail. Is this something we do as teachers?

Parents too are guilty of this bias, and experience from Parent Consultations where a student will gain high marks in all subjects but one, which becomes the focus of the meeting, are common. This is from the viewpoint of a parent as well as a teacher.

---

[6] Gonzalez–Jensen, Margarita, and Norma Sadler. "Behind Closed Doors: Status Quo Bias in Read Aloud Selections." *Equity and Excellence in Education* 30.1 (1997): 27-31.

Macabre Constant

This is a relatively new term, explored by André Antibi, which suggested that teachers and lecturers subconsciously assumed three groups of ability within any group - high, medium and low, no matter the actual ability of the group themselves. This creates an artificial failure of students, carried out by the adjustment of tests to filter to these groups rather than testing knowledge and skills[7].

Reflect on your own practice; have you ever included trickier questions in a test paper to cater for the higher ability, rather than seeing what knowledge/skills you had taught had been effectively retained? If you have, than the Macabre Constant is a bias you really should be familiar with in a more intimate manner[8].

Publication Bias

We are largely hungry animals for new information, ideas and practices as teachers, but would be wise to view our diet of literature using the lens of publication bias. There is a certain diet which publishers and course providers feed, and this is based on interest as well as need, thus perpetuating publication bias. Take as an example the term Outstanding. Introduced by OFSTED in 2009 as the highest of its four Inspection categories in England[9], this word quickly grew in popularity.

---

[7] *Les Notes : La fin du cauchemar: Ou en finir avec la constante macabre* by André Antibi, Antibi, 2007

[8] "Macabre constant " <https://en.wikipedia.org/wiki/Macabre_constant>

[9] "Ofsted" <https://en.wikipedia.org/wiki/Ofsted>

Indeed, research into its prevalence in the United Kingdom showed strong growth roughly two years after its introduction[10], where the use of Outstanding in other English-speaking country searches showed static use. This extended to Publishing houses and Educational suppliers, where using 'Outstanding' has almost come to represent *"this will get you through a successful inspection."* For the sake of disclosure, I should admit to doing this myself[11].

Cognitive Bias

This is perhaps the most commonly-known types of bias, demonstrated in patterns of illogical judgement, based around an perception of social reality. In reality, it is the brain's way of using rules of thumb to make decisions and inform our life. In the book *Freakonomics*[12] for example, it was shown that swimming pools killed more children in the US than handguns. This is at odds with our available information, assumptions (pools are good, guns are bad), and even the lack of statistical data to support this argument available to us. The statement has an impact precisely due to our cognitive biases toward both pools and guns. Cognitive Bias covers a much wider area, taking into account many of the areas covered in this section, but can be seen as the umbrella term for irrationality. It is also notoriously difficult to correct, especially in view of the range of addictions supported by irrational thoughts. One area of exploration in cognitive psychology has had the most

---

[10] https://www.google.com/trends/explore#q=outstanding&geo=GB&cmpt=q&tz=Etc%2FGMT-1

[11] *"100 Ideas for Primary Teachers: Outstanding Teaching"* by Stephen Lockyer, Bloomsbury, 2015

[12] "Freakonomics" by Steven D. Levitt, Stephen J. Dubner, HarperCollins, 2011

success when those with a cognitive bias are held fully accountable for their attributions[13].

Cognitive bias can be seen within an Education setting in a macro or micro environment - from Education Ministers pushing forward proposals on the basis of their own schooling experiences rather than grounded research, to teachers refusing to use more appropriate means to deliver lessons.

To blame everything on cognitive bias however is to stand by a fire rather than trying to put it out or discover what caused the fire in the first place. It is easy to rally against what could be simply described as human nature, but genuine impact is made when someone stands and says, "so what can we do about it?"

Observer Bias

No overview of bias in a book about education would be complete without examination of the observer bias, and this is included as an important bias to be aware of in our surroundings rather than a politicised rant against observation of teachers or students in the classroom (where, interestingly, one seems legitimate and the other morally wrong).

Although this dovetails with confirmation bias, observer bias technically is better described as the *observer-expectancy effect*, where the observer directly or indirectly influences those being observed to confirm their own hypotheses, sometimes ignoring adverse information.

---

[13] Skitka, Linda J, Kathleen Mosier, and Mark D Burdick. "Accountability and automation bias." *International Journal of Human-Computer Studies* 52.4 (2000): 701-717.

A similar bias can be seen in the *Hawthorne Effect*, where participants behave differently due the very act of being observed. How often do we change when teaching and a visitor walks in? We in effect start delivering the type of teaching we believe they would expect to see. Even aware of this, I have noticed that I tend to 'liven up' with another adult in the classroom, speaking louder, clearer and with more enunciation. I am effectively presenting a better me, when my students should be getting a better me as a matter of course.

Attribution Bias

This is a common bias within Education, and is essentially a judgement made around someone based our own beliefs or assumptions. Those situations where we are frustrated by someone's behaviour because we wouldn't do it that way is a classic example of attribution bias.

These judgements can impede collegiality, damage working relationships and also encourage the silo-like nature of teaching both within a setting and in a wider nature. This bias even threads back to biblical misattribution; "treat others as you would like to be treated," should logically read, "treat others as *they* would like to be treated."

Before doom and gloom sets in, there is hope! It has been found that attributional retraining can have a positive academic impact among students, especially where there is a recognition that internal factors have more effect than external factors (or excuses). Put simply, this correlates well with the recent growth in interest surrounding Mindset, and acknowledges that taking responsibility for self-influence rather than investing in a blame culture creates a more sustainable student outlook[14].

There is an awful lot to contend with when considering all the bias we may experience, or even demonstrate ourselves through our teaching. Some teachers are more aware of these habits than others, but awareness that they even exist is important.

Consider for the moment the last three important decisions you made. What or who had a bias on those decisions; were they genuinely down to free will or independent thought, or were you influenced by other means?

---

[14] Perry, Raymond P, and Kurt S Penner. "Enhancing academic achievement in college students through attributional retraining and instruction." *Journal of Educational Psychology* 82.2 (1990): 262.

5. Stop doing, start thinking

This is not a call-to-arms about giving up the automatic pilot which guides so much of our waking thoughts, so much as an active growth in awareness that aspects are subconscious, and require both reflection and examination.

We should always be questioning, searching for the 'why?' of our motivations and drives. The difficulty is, this can be tough thinking, so instead we relegate this to a more cogitative endeavour, waiting almost for the answers to surface, fully-formed in our minds.

This can happen of course, and we allow confirmation bias to encourage the thought that this happens far more often than we would actually recognise it to happen.

Metacognition - thinking about thinking - is this process. It is giving considered, dedicated time to exploring how and why we think the way we that we do, and formulating ideas which try to be free from our routines, biases and patterns.

This type of thinking also explores the way to solve problems in unique or unfamiliar experiences. One particular problem for technology is something we as humans manage in microseconds; crowd sizes. Despite much research, CCTV technology can only go some way to estimating crowd sizes in the way humans are able to infer this even with peripheral glances (take deciding where to stand at a tube station, and our scanning ability when the tube actually arrives for example).

The biggest hurdle is in understanding the process that the human mind utilises to carry this estimation out. For something so seemingly simple, it's actually incredibly hard to describe, let alone program, in a simple enough fashion that a digital entity can accurately manage[15]. Estimating crowd sizes is almost instinctual, and there is the blurry line between full and overcrowded, with us able to perceive this in a way which can't be broken down easily.

So what can be broken down into stages that can be easily understood? How does this help us to think? One of the easiest ways of exploring this is to ask a robot to make a sandwich. If you don't have a robot handy, you might want to ask Phil Bagge...

[15] "The Curious Science of Counting a Crowd." <http://www.popularmechanics.com/science/a7121/the-curious-science-of-counting-a-crowd/>

6. That is illogical

How can making a sandwich help with thinking about thinking? For some children, this simple process is easily unpacked, although the robot is frighteningly realistic.

Phil Bagge is a teacher, passionate about teaching key computer skills and logic, and generously sharing his tips, strategies and even videos of how to make this more explicit for his charges[16].

In one of many clips he has recorded, he teaches logical sequencing, carrying this out by asking the children to create instructions to guide the children to help a robot make a jam sandwich for them. Phil 'plays' the robot guide, a digital savant which simply carries out exactly what is requested - no more or less than this. Watching the robot follow their instructions highlights for the children the number of assumed stages that they have not recorded for the robot to carry out. It takes progressive edits and rewrites to ensure that the robot follows all the steps completely, and highlights in a clear way the manner in which all thinking needs to be shared, and not assumed, in order for the robot to succeed the task.

This is computational thinking at its most raw - logic exposed. By making the process conscious (written down) and visible (in the demonstration), areas which had been missed are highlighted. In

---

[16] "Jam Sandwich - YouTube."<http://www.youtube.com/watch?v=NaRrq2q9-el>

doing so, the children are exploring a stage in the metacognition process, shown in the model below.

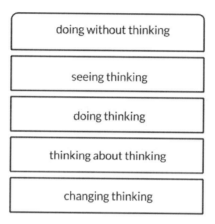

doing without thinking

seeing thinking

doing thinking

thinking about thinking

changing thinking

In this lesson, the children are beginning to see their thinking exposed. They are also witnessing their thinking being carried out. It is fascinating, and made all the more effective by having such a thoughtless process made thought*ful*. It is this process which metacognition seeks to encourage. But before we look at how and why metacognition is such a powerful influence within teaching and learning, it is worth looking at one more of the villains of non-thinking; the dilemma cul-de-sac.

7. Knowing what to do

Solving the purpose of Education is a tricky aim for any book.

One definition however fits most comfortably into any exploration of metacognition, first coined by Jean Piaget, and is primarily about intelligence rather than education itself:

"Knowing what to do when you don't know what to do"

This is my teaching leitmotif, and one which I turn to constantly, to admittedly varying degrees of success if I am honest. I recently observed some students at the end of a test, when I'd told them when complete, to "check through their work." My frustration grew as I watched them turning pages in their test booklet, scanning through the questions and their answers. This was checking in the lightest of senses.

My frustration quickly redirected when it struck me that I'd never explained fully or modelled what checking a test paper was. For them, it was clearly 'see if I've missed any out,' a world away from actively checking the paper for errors, misunderstandings or places where answers could be expanded. Checking had no definition for them, so they were giving me their interpretation of checking; busyness.

Here were intelligent students, who had been placed in an understanding cul-de-sac, and without the confidence in front of their peers to put their hands up and ask, "what do you mean by that?"

Metacognition aims to improve this perspective by not only encouraging thinking skills, but thinking about situations where they don't know what to do next, *and make active decisions to correct this position*. Without giving the students this key guidance, we run the risk of regularly putting them in situations for which they have no experience, which is good, but without the training in order to work out their next steps, which is bad.

8. Those subtle changes

We talk in Education about building up strong relationships with students, but could our tacit nature be inhibiting our ability know them better?

There is some research which shows the longer we know someone, in some ways the less we know about them, due to entrenched assumptions.[17] In an experiment, people were asked to rate 118 items on a scale of 1 (dislike) to 4 (like a lot), predicting how much someone else would like them. The research found that those who knew the person fared much better in their accuracy than those who were predicting for complete strangers. So far, so understandable.

What the researchers found however was that the longer you knew someone you were predicting for, the *less* accurate you were! Part of this decline was suggested to be down to the efforts made at the start of a relationship with another person, where you are consciously getting to know them. Over time, this effort is reduced, and you end up starting to fill in the gaps. The researchers also suggested that over time, changes in attitudes and preferences are less likely to be spotted, especially if they are subtle changes.

I like to play a game with menus at restaurants to see if the people I am with can predict what I'm likely to choose. I pretend that this

---

[17] Scheibehenne, Benjamin, Jutta Mata, and Peter M Todd. "Older but not wiser–Predicting a partner's preferences gets worse with age." *Journal of Consumer Psychology* 21.2 (2011): 184-191.

is a test to see if they really know me, but it's actually that I'm awful at selecting something, so will often run with their suggestion. By and large, friends and family score quite a high ratio, but this can be thrown. I was recently introduced to Halloumi cheese and, never having had it before, now tend to notice it on lots of menus. This is of course not known to everyone, so they might not suggest this at all.

The similarity with our students, and even with our fellow teaching staff, is strong. Each year, we welcome new classes and make judgements on them, either with previous information, or building up a snapshot of them in the initial lessons. This then can form the backbone of our viewpoint. When a student unexpectedly completes some work in a way that we couldn't have predicted, is it that that potential was always there and unseen, or has some event happened which we justify as accounting for this change?

Within our relationships with students and staff, there are many actions and events which can subtly (or dramatically) change their attitudes, drives and preferences. We can be aware of these in some respects, but it is a danger not to actively explore these more carefully.

If this seems unfair, think of the new member of staff who joins you, questioning everything. This approach often bristles, but what they are doing is actually comparing what has subtly evolved over time in a new (to them) setting, compared to their old setting. While their approach might need some work, any procedure which can be prefixed with, *"we've always done it this way,"* is part of your setting's tacit nature. Sometimes the nudge is a good thing.

9. Anchor's Away

How much of what you do, think and feel is purely free choice, and how much is given over to subtle anchors in your environment; prompts which adjust your perspective, outlook and decision-making without you even realising?

Supermarkets are incredibly canny about this, carefully orchestrating prices so that the premium price is in your eyeline, which in turn gives you an anchor of that variety of item (making you compare prices against this, rather than a price you consider to be fair for the product). This is such a crucial area for retailers, they employ *plangrammers*[18], whose job is to calculate the optimal arrangement of products on the shelves in order to maximise profits.

The supermarket is filled with anchors; test this out by writing a shopping list next time you get some groceries, and be as specific as you can about quantities and weights. Count the number of times you are tempted to change your mind about a product or add an item not on your list into your trolley. You'll finish amazed at how manipulated you actually are.

In another example, it was noted by researchers that donations to hurricane disasters increased if they shared the same name, or

---

[18] "What is planogram? - Definition from WhatIs.com." <http://whatis.techtarget.com/definition/planogram>

even initial![19] We become more interested in someone with the most tenuous of links to ourselves, and this can affect our judgement whether consciously or not.

One experiment I've carried out a number of times in a range of contexts is to ask those I'm with to write down the last two digits of their mobile number. I then ask them to give a price for an item I bought on eBay, which was between £1-£100. Finally, they take the smaller number from the larger number. Despite differences in group size, age range or gender, over 50% end up with a number 10 or lower - the first (arbitrary) number acting as a mental anchor for the second price guesstimate.

The difficulty with mental anchors is the same as with physical anchors; they are often hard to see, and even harder to shift. You may stray a little from them, but you are effectively tethered until you make the conscious effort to remove your position.

It is this deliberate removal of the anchor which we aim to do with metacognition. By acknowledging that we are thinking or feeling in a certain way, we are also highlighting that some thinking has gone on which is worth examining and exploring further.

[19] Chandler, Jesse, Tiffany M. Griffin, and Nicholas Sorensen. "In the "I" of the storm: Shared initials increase disaster donations." Judgment and Decision Making 3.5 (2008): 404-410.

10. The big meta research sleeper hit

The growth in popularity and interest in metacognition within Education came to a certain degree when this relatively unfamiliar term started appearing near the top of some low-cost, high-impact teaching methods, primarily as a result of meta research by several bodies.

It was so unfamiliar that the byline 'thinking about thinking' became synonymous with it. John Hattie's work in Educational meta research[20] highlighted this as being a superb intervention in assisting learning, and one which teachers could implement both quickly (next lesson) and in a macro level (in your classroom). Everyone likes a panacea, and compared to other methods with a similar effect size[21] (the system normally used to measure the impact over a range of research findings), needed little if any funding, special equipment or extra staff.

---

[20] Hattie, John. Visible learning: A synthesis of over 800 meta-analyses relating to achievement. Routledge, 2013.

[21] Orwin, Robert G. "A fail-safe N for effect size in meta-analysis." *Journal of educational statistics* (1983): 157-159.

In *Visible Learning and the Science of How We Learn*[22], Hattie explored research which examined a range of influences on learning, underlining that it was not a complete methodology on 'how to teach,' but a collection of the most relevant and statistically accurate summaries of the research carried out thus far. His follow-up book, *Visible Learning for Teachers*[23] highlighted more overtly the impact which metacognition and self-regulation (the process of taking control of and evaluating one's own learning and behaviour) could have a discernible impact.

In it, Hattie more deeply explores the notion of metacognition and self-regulation, with the most current effect size being listed as 0.69[24], the base mark of 0.40 indicating a standard effect size over one year. Put simply, effective cognition can impact students by almost another nine months in one school year. More importantly, a lot of metacognitive strategies don't show up in end-of-year results, but their effect is instead seen in sustained results in following years. This then is the definition of intervention - giving a sustainable impact rather than a quick fix.

Of course, averages hide a lot of ills - if I froze one of my feet and set fire to the other, on average they'd be warm. Within the analysis, it highlights that some metacognitive interventions have a small effect size (the effects of note taking has an ES of 0.22) while others are more dramatic (memory training programs have an ES of 1.28).

[22] Hattie, John, and Gregory CR Yates. *Visible learning and the science of how we learn*. Routledge, 2013.

[23] Hattie, John. *Visible learning for teachers: Maximizing impact on learning*. Routledge, 2012.

[24] http://visible-learning.org/hattie-ranking-influences-effect-sizes-learning-achievement/

What this book aims to distill are the beneficial products of all ranges in the effect size spectrum;

- Where there was a high effect size, what this was down to, and how this could be implemented in everyday practice
- Where there was a low effect size, an exploration of why this could be the case, and what lessons could be learnt

One of the attracting factors of metacognition is that it is a bootstrap teaching strategy - with little to no cost involved in implementation. By its very nature, the intangibility of the process can make it both hard to justify and actively develop. Externally, all school stakeholders can see money being spent on new equipment, staff or remedial programmes.

Anything based entirely within a classroom relies upon a teacher buying into the concept, using it correctly, and if necessary, demonstrating the difference it makes to their students. This can inherently be a tough sell to teachers, especially those who for a number of reasons may be entrenched in their pedagogical belief. For that reason, building confidence in using metacognition in classes is one of the aims of this book.

11. In Sutton we Trust

This was a view shared by the Sutton Trust Teaching and Learning Toolkit[25], a system designed by the charity to help schools sift through the huge volumes of research in Education which indicated what teaching and learning methods were best for interventionist purposes.

Originally designed to help schools decide to what to invest their Pupil Premium money in for their students, it quickly became a useful go-to guide for all staff and schools, helping them to drill down and explore educational research under three guiding principles:

- What works well (and doesn't);
- What costs lots (and what doesn't); and
- What research there has been (or hasn't).

The toolkit gave any member of staff presenting to their board of Governors a firm pedagogical backbone to support their case for

---

[25] "Sutton Trust - Teaching and Learning Toolkit." <http://www.suttontrust.com/about-us/education-endowment-foundation/teaching-learning-toolkit/>

x or y, and was rebranded the Teaching and Learning toolkit[26]. If an intervention programme (as that is what the Pupil Premium funds were for originally) can make a discernible difference to some students, why not spread this impact among all students? This appeared to be the Trust's view too.

The Toolkit seems even more effusive in its praise of Metacognition and self-regulation. Splitting research into 30 different topics, metacognition was identified as having one of the lowest intervention costs (1 out of 5 on their scale), some of the most secure research bases (4 out of 5), with a projected gain of 8 months[27]. Measured against cost, it has the highest gain alongside Feedback. Measured against research strength, it also has the highest score, with only one intervention (Phonics) above it, which itself is quite age-specific and has an estimated gain of only four months. In short, metacognition is the diamond of the toolkit crown - not much else comes close.

So, what do the combined meta-research analyses give us? Certainly a confidence that metacognition can make a difference; an opportunity to effectively offer a school-wide intervention at an incredibly low cost compared to other interventions (The Sutton Trust estimates this as around £80 per student, roughly equivalent to the take-home pay of one Teaching Assistant for one day), and if nothing else, a set of robust, evidence-based guiding principles to use metacognition and self-regulation principles in the classroom.

---

[26] http://www.suttontrust.com/about-us/education-endowment-foundation/teaching-learning-toolkit/

[27] https://educationendowmentfoundation.org.uk/toolkit/toolkit-a-z/

12. Guiding principles

Before diving into the techniques themselves, the research indicates a much wider set of guiding principles, where using these techniques can be seen as far more effective when used against the propositions. These are explored further in this book, but they provide a robust foundation for the various strategies outlined elsewhere. They are;

Implementation is more effective in non-intensive, small group situations

Research found that small group implementation was more successful than whole class or one-to-one strategies.[28] This was most productive when combined with a less intensive program. The estimated average length of a programme has been suggested to be 12 lessons of around 40 minutes[29].- Principle ES 0.67

Thinking Programmes have more impact than 'gestures'

---

[28] Chiu, Chris WT. "Synthesizing Metacognitive Interventions: What Training Characteristics Can Improve Reading Performance?." (1998).

[29] Scruggs, Thomas E., et al. "Do special education interventions improve learning of secondary content? A meta-analysis." Remedial and Special Education 31.6 (2010): 437-449.

Extensive research has found that introducing thinking in a programme format makes a large difference upon impact. Some papers noted that these types of programmes had taught the students how to learn.[30] Research also noted that there are variations according to gender, age and subject. Principle ES 0.74

Thinking skills are not a quick fix

A study concerned with improving writing over the transition from Primary to Secondary followed a set procedure, with an extended work focus and was built with both teachers and guidance from language experts, over at least a term and a half[31]. A specific focus helped to target self regulation to that one area, but one transferable strand was self-scoring and peer scoring. Principle ES 0.74

The aim of teaching self-regulation is to build self-teaching strategies

One meta-research study identified that the most effective metacognitive strategy was the use of self-questioning with students[32]. This, combined with reinforcement from the teacher had the largest measurable difference. - Principle ES 0.71

The teacher is key in developing metacognitive processes

----

[30] Higgins, Steve, et al. "A meta-analysis of the impact of the implementation of thinking skills approaches on pupils." (2005).

[31] https://educationendowmentfoundation.org.uk/uploads/pdf/ EEF_Evaluation_Report_-_Improving_Writing_Quality_- _May_2014_v2.pdf

[32] Haller, Eileen P., David A. Child, and Herbert J. Walberg. "Can comprehension be taught? A quantitative synthesis of "metacognitive" studies." Educational researcher 17.9 (1988): 5-8.

Just as you are able to use a saw without instruction but expert guidance can refine your sawing technique, teacher input, especially at the beginning of an instructional process, is vital[33]. In order to start thinking about thinking, techniques need to be shared. In the cited research, the introduction of pegwords and keywords with some lower-ability students had a dramatic impact. Principle - ES 1.62

Setting of self-goals, and adjusting these, is essential

In order to avoid what Benz & Schmitz term as 'learning disorientation,' students need to be taught how to set themselves learning goals, plan their work, and adjust these goals accordingly during the process[34]. It is in this adjustment process that students avoid tangenting their learning away from their own goals, and requires discipline in order to succeed. Principle - ES 0.78

Learning difficulties are related to not knowing how to learn effectively

This is a key principle, highlighted in meta-research conducted by Kim et al. They found a relationship between those students who were underperforming academically and understanding how to

---

[33] Mastropieri, Margo A., and Thomas E. Scruggs. "Constructing more meaningful relationships: Mnemonic instruction for special populations." Educational Psychology Review 1.2 (1989): 83-111.

[34] Scholl, Philipp, et al. "Implementation and Evaluation of a Tool for setting Goals in self-regulated Learning with Web Resources." Learning in the Synergy of Multiple Disciplines. Springer Berlin Heidelberg, 2009. 521-534.

learn[35]. By teaching these students effective learning strategies, the gains upon grades were dramatic. Principle - ES 0.96

A range of metacognitive and self-regulation strategies should be employed

While there might be favoured strategies for different subjects, in order for students to gain the most from metacognitive strategies, a wide range should be used (with the caveat that some have a greater or lesser effect, and that some strategies were less researched than others)[36].

Among the recommended strategies were: Mnemonic strategies (ES=1.47); Spatial or Graphic Organizers (ES=0.93); Classroom Learning Strategies (ES=1.11); Computer-Assisted Instruction (ES=0.63); Study Aids (ES=0.94); Hands-On or Activity-Oriented Learning (ES=0.63) and Explicit instruction (ES=1.68). Principle - ES 1.00

It may seem that these principles have been cherry-picked for their effectiveness; this is because they have been. All will be explored further, or examples given in relation to these principles. Where an effect size is low, this is also examined, with lessons learned or discussion around why the effect size might be low.

------

[35] Kim, Dongil, et al. "Effects of cognitive learning strategies for Korean learners: A meta-analysis." Asia Pacific Education Review 9.4 (2008): 409-422.

[36] Scruggs, Thomas E., et al. "Do special education interventions improve learning of secondary content? A meta-analysis." Remedial and Special Education 31.6 (2010): 437-449.

13. The age of metacognition

If metacognition and self-regulation techniques are important, when should they be taught in schools?

There is robust evidence that preschool language (and especially conversation) both between peers and between adults and children will influence children's access to cognitive strategies. What is more clear in the research however is that although children aged 4-5 do demonstrate techniques of memorisation and orientation, they do not particularly influence recall performance until aged 6 and up. They can begin to make use of deliberate techniques for remembering, but until then, there is only a slow growth in intentionality with recall.

It is hard to read the last paragraph without considering anecdotal evidence to draw upon; my eldest son for example could recognise almost every car logo aged two, but it is important to emphasise that research is often based around testing a specific skill or technique against a set criteria, in order to normalise results.

There is a noticeable change in technique as children get older, from a passive effort to a more active method, and changes have also been identified in rehearsal, organisation and elaboration. What is interesting is that these describe normal habits - there is no reason why memorisation techniques can't be learned by someone younger, leading to greater recall[37]. Recall was improved further with a visual prompt, such as a picture of the items needing to be remembered. In studies where younger children were given help in learning a new technique, scaffolding was the primary tool used.

It should be noted however that although children might be able to highlight a memorisation technique articulately, they may not use it in practice. This indicates a need for teachers to continually share technique opportunities before, during and after a task[38]. The reverse can also be true, with children using a technique, but not being aware it is a technique at all[39]. Their meta-memory (active awareness they are using a memory strategy) has not been recognised consciously. Part of a teacher's role then is also to highlight good strategy use even when a student is not aware that

---

[37] Ornstein, Peter A et al. "Retrieving for rehearsal: An analysis of active rehearsal in children's memory." *Developmental Psychology* 21.4 (1985): 633.

[38] Sodian, Beate, Wolfgang Schneider, and Marion Perlmutter. "Recall, clustering, and metamemory in young children." *Journal of Experimental Child Psychology* 41.3 (1986): 395-410.

[39] Bjorklund, David F, and Barbara R Zeman. "Children's organization and metamemory awareness in their recall of familiar information." *Child Development* (1982): 799-810.

they are using one[40]. Indeed, doing this leads to greater performance[41].

Before memory comes understanding; given a list of technical words linked to your profession and a list of Ukrainian cooking words, which are more likely to be easily rehearsed and remembered? Likewise, the growth in memory among older children also reflects their growing understanding of the world. For any metacognition technique to be successful, there should be a purposeful, visible context for the students.

---

[40] I recognised that I was using the Keyword technique whilst citing the researchers Bjorklund and Seman above, carrying their names in my head as Bjork Land and semen. Apologies.

[41] Schneider, Wolfgang et al. "The development of young children's memory strategies: First findings from the Würzburg Longitudinal Memory Study." *Journal of Experimental Child Psychology* 88.2 (2004): 193-209.

14. Developing cognitive orientation

There has been an increase in the debate over whether skills or knowledge should lead in any curriculum; not so much that both should co-exist, but which is more important.

Within skills is the need for transferability. If a student learns to analyse a text in English, the multitude of benefits for other subjects is high. Learning a skill discretely may be appropriate for certain subjects, but the principle of transferable skills is one which can't be neglected.

This is a point raised in research[42] which recognised that students who were able to more flexibly choose strategies to meet the needs of the task fared better. As a by-product, they were also better able to adjust their techniques, and make monitor the success of their efforts. This is the cognitive orientation from the section title - the ability to draw from a range of strategies. It follows that the more strategies students have at their disposal (which they are confident of using), the more opportunities they may also have to orientate more successfully.

---

[42] Ornstein, PA et al. "Linking the classroom context and the development of children's memory skills." *Handbook of research on schools, schooling, and human development* (2010): 42-59.

This also highlights the need for all staff to 'buy in' on metacognitive strategies, and indeed share both their instruction and use of them with students, and also to highlight or scaffold opportunities for them to be used in class. The difficulty with this is multi-stranded however. How can you track which students have been taught which strategy (and if they are competent and comfortable with using it)? Are staff sufficiently confident to actively teach these strategies, and inform students of when they might be best to use the strategies?

Too often, innovation is often only accepted if familiar[43], and this, combined with the silo-like nature of our working practices in Education at times (although the growth of Social Media and blogging use is beginning to challenge this) makes this task much harder. Perhaps this is the reason why, despite its research impact, metacognition isn't a central thread of our education system?

---

[43] "Familiar Innovation" - a phrase created by my friend Eylan Ezekiel

15. Trapped in the diffusion curve

There are several ways for an idea to become imbedded in a school culture. One is to have it enforced upon you, such as Interactive Whiteboards in UK schools.

This was done with a great deal of fanfare and at enormous expense. The value of this investment has been widely debated both in classrooms and in scholarly research articles, but the evidence is fairly clear - in the Sutton Trust's Teaching and Learning Toolkit, the amount these costs do not represent particularly good value for money[44].

The relative failure of Interactive Whiteboards could be viewed as two-fold; that they were enforced rather than desired, and that there was very little training provided for such a classroom-dominating technology. That they fit the 'solution for a problem which doesn't exist' could of course also be argued.

Other changes in the implementation of school culture and pedagogy follow the more familiar path of the diffusion of innovation, as made famous by the book of the same name[45], which is now more often seen to describe the success rates (or otherwise) of startup companies and Apps.

---

[44] https://educationendowmentfoundation.org.uk/toolkit/toolkit-a-z/digital-technology/

[45] Rogers, Everett M. *Diffusion of innovations*. Simon and Schuster, 2010.

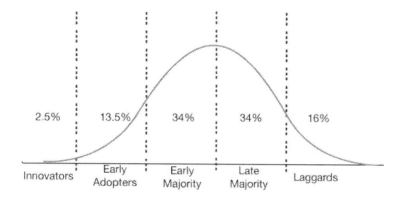

As you can see from the graph, the innovators make up just 2.5% of innovation, and their zionic calling often attracts that next group of Early Adopters.

If we examine this against the earlier statistic that roughly 2% of lesson time is devoted to memorisation techniques and metacognition, it does make one wonder if metacognition is trapped inside a niche bubble currently, with very little opportunity for natural growth.

This could be attributed to two key reasons. First, that it is quite hidden in terms of classroom practice and pedagogy. It would be hard to miss a new Interactive Whiteboard (or its use), whereas metacognitive techniques are more interwoven in the fabric of a lesson.

Secondly, the payoff of teaching these techniques is traditionally over a long period of time. It is hard to encourage big impact when the truth is that impact occurs slowly. There is a patience inherent with believing metacognition can make a discernible difference, and patience is a commodity which can be ill-afforded in today's educational climate. Any active metacognition practitioner therefore bears some responsibility not only to innovate their practice, but also to share the myriad successes with those staff who are potentially early-adopters.

MEMORY

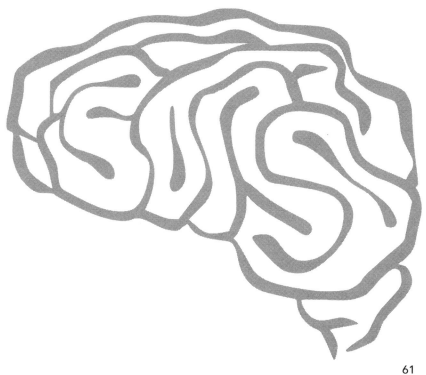

16. Mnemonic Strategies

Ask any UK Primary School child when Guy Fawkes tried to blow up the Houses of Parliament and they will be able to name the date. Conveniently, Guido Fawkes chose a date which was syllabically helpful and also rhymed with the word 'remember.'

The same could be said for the colours of the rainbow, and the use of 'i before e,' although the latter rhyme is a blunt tool, with a range of exceptions[46]. These are all mnemonic strategies for recalling facts; hooks to aid recall.

Metacognition in this sense takes two forms; both to teach facts using these strategies, but also to encourage students to develop their own mnemonic strategies which they can employ independently.

So why are some things hard to remember, and yet other facts and trivia seem to be locked into our memories forever?

Mnemonic strategies work best for facts, procedures and details which are high in quantity, unfamiliar, have a high level of abstractness, or complexity; very often they can have a combination of these! Names for example can be notoriously hard

---

[46] "I before E except after C" <https://en.wikipedia.org/wiki/I_before_E_except_after_C>

to remember for a variety of reasons, not least because they don't actually have any meaning. Anecdotally however, it seems easier to recall someone's name if it is a name familiar to you; the hook is already there[47].

Yet, as Hattie recognises, this is perhaps one of the strongest paradoxes in Education (emphasis my own):

"...although teachers make it plain that they expect students to accurately remember information, there is surprisingly little instruction taking place about how to remember. Students might be told to remember, but appear to receive almost no guidance in how to remember.[48]"

Hattie draws on this viewpoint from a study by Moely & Hart[49] which found that teaching memorisation techniques occurred for just 2% of teaching time, and at no point at all for 10% of observed lessons. Perhaps these teachers had more faith in the

----

[47] "Everyone is biased: Harvard professor's work reveals we ..." <http://www.boston.com/news/science/blogs/science-in-mind/2013/02/05/everyone-biased-harvard-professor-work-reveals-barely-know-our-own-minds/7x5K4gvrvaT5d3vpDaXC1K/blog.html>

48 Hattie, John. Visible learning: A synthesis of over 800 meta-analyses relating to achievement. Routledge, 2013.

[49] Moely, Barbara E., et al. "The teacher's role in facilitating memory and study strategy development in the elementary school classroom." Child Development 63.3 (1992): 653-672.

'jelly flinging' technique of learning - repeat it over and over until it sticks. This, as we can all testify, only works in a limited number of situations. Indeed, my phone camera memory is dotted with poorly-angled snaps of my car registration plate for different purposes. This is a seven-character string I see every day, yet it will not remain in my mind, because I've given no effort to memorise it.

Further research[50] revealed that we expect students to carry out some form of memory work in around 50% of lesson time, although instructions for how to do this appeared only 5% of the time.

Children naturally have an understanding of having to remember something, even at a young age. Given toys to recall after playing with them, four-year-olds in a study played differently, and less, with them[51]. Again, we are entrusting children to use their own methods to remember facts, details, *things*, using their own techniques, which are likely to be blunt and only mildly effective. The approach seen by those in the recall group does suggest that you need to be in a specific learning state in order to start remembering something. Is this something we do in our classroom?

It is unsurprising that mnemonic techniques have themselves become mnemonics, helping us both to remember them and to

---

[50] Ornstein, PA et al. "Linking the classroom context and the development of children's memory skills." *Handbook of research on schools, schooling, and human development* (2010): 42-59.

[51] Baker-Ward, Lynne, Peter A Ornstein, and Debra J Holden. "The expression of memorization in early childhood." *Journal of Experimental Child Psychology* 37.3 (1984): 555-575.

pass this on to students. What then is the the process of creating a Mnemonic? Enter the three R process[52]:

- Recoding - the freedom to adjust the data in any way
- Relating - creating hooks to make the data far more relatable
- Retrieving - ensuring the hook is simple enough to be recalled itself

This is the basis for any good mnemonic system. Make it your own, using a hook, and have easy access to that hook. Used with recall of foreign words for example, there is a dramatically higher level of recall. When used with cartoons or illustrations, there is an even higher level of recall, and this carries from younger children and initial letter sounds, through to older children learning foreign or technical words. The use of keyword and pegword techniques are successful for lists (and are explained in further pages).

There is an interesting offshoot to the research into mnemonics; most work was done with students who struggled in some way academically. The success they felt with the memory techniques they learnt appeared to improve their academic self-worth - they felt that they *could* achieve.

---

[52] Levin, Joel R. "Pictorial strategies for school learning: Practical illustrations." *Cognitive strategy research* (1983): 213-237.

17. Peg Words

Even the term induces an image of perhaps a washing line with pegs on it, objects hanging from them, yet the simplicity of the term disguises just how powerful this technique is for memory recall.

For one interview, and given the freedom to teach a lesson on anything, I taught the trial class this system. Under the guise of learning a random shopping list of items (newspaper, thermometer, mirror, bag of soil etc), I actually surreptitiously taught them the order of the planets, which I revealed near the end of the lesson.

There was a magical moment when the children realised that they had learnt the order of the planets without even mentioning the planets themselves. Testament to that method, and I'll admit that I have a bias as the lesson is imprinted in my memory more than the 10,000+ other lessons I've taught in my career thus far, is that I can still recall the order.

Also known as the hook system, it requires a little deliberate memorisation beforehand, luckily assisted with rhyme. Here is the chart you'll need to know by heart in order to utilise the method:

1	2	3	4	5	6	7	8	9	10
bun	shoe	tree	door	hive	sticks	heaven	gate	wine	hen

Hopefully you are able to see at a glance that each object rhymes with the number. If you know the numbers one to ten, you should be able to look away now and recall this list. The first part of this task is complete.

Although this method works particularly well for ordered lists, it works just as well for lists of 'things' - features of global warming for example (where order is not important). In my lesson mentioned above, I used this method to learn two lists - one explicit and the other revealed in the final stages.

Here then is the method: for each item on your list, create a visual illustration connecting the peg word to the shopping list item (in this example). For *sun-newspaper* one could imagine a newspaper bursting into flames, or the Sun wearing shades and reading a newspaper. The more visually-unusual the image, the better it seems to work.

One key aspect of this method is that this stage needs to be done using full, dedicated concentration. I have found that students can be wildly creative with their illustrations, and this is especially useful for bedding in the memory, since there is ownership.

Once each image has been 'imprinted,' test it out by saying the order, backward and forward several times, and ask someone to test you, starting the order at a specific place, or giving the answer to a selected number. You'll be surprised at how well you can recall the items.

One charm of this method is that it can work for a multitude of lists - the pegs seem to give themselves freely rather than cling limpet-like to one list, resistant to change. Try this method with the list overleaf.

The next stage of my lesson involved a 'reveal' that the students had also learnt the order of the planets. This utilised the keyword method, especially popular for technical and foreign language memory improvement. Explained in more depth shortly, it is simply altering a word to be learnt into something similar-sounding, hopefully encapsulated into an image or phrase.

Peg Word	Shopping List (explicit)	Order of planets (hidden)
bun	newspaper	Sun
shoe	thermometer	Mercury
tree	mirror	Venus
door	bag of soil	Earth
hive	chocolate bar	Mars
sticks	skipping rope	Jupiter
heaven	fine cloth	Saturn
gate	toilet paper	Uranus
wine	recorder	Neptune
hen	dog toy	Pluto

For the planet example, I began with three/tree/mirror, and conjured up the image of a mirror tree, with different mirrors growing from the various branches. Using the key word technique, I linked mirrors to Venus by saying that people who used mirrors a lot were very vain. Doing this for all the items of the shopping list and the planets took around two minutes, yet were instantly recalled.

Some caveats: I am aware that the Sun is not a planet, but included it to help with the right order (outward in the Solar System). Likewise, Pluto has been downgraded but I was being inclusive.

The Peg Word method has several variants which can also be explored:

- Numeral Pegs - the most popular of these is the very clever Major system, described in the next section.
- Pictorial Pegs - Using just images for the shapes of the numbers, this seems to my mind to potentially over-complicate the simplicity, but some students may prefer to use the shapes of numbers to aid them instead. Some suggestions include a stick to represent 1, a swan to represent 2, a bent wire to represent 3 and so on.
- Beyond 10 - There are several different lists of pegwords up to 100 (and some up to 1000) online to aid anyone wishing to memorise a list beyond 10. For brevity, here are 11 to 20.

There is quite a jump to recall these as easily as the first 10 peg words, and I would be inclined, especially at Primary level, to keep with the 1-10 list.

11	12	13	14	15
Cricket	dozen	hurting	courting	lifting
16	17	18	19	20
licking	beckoning	waiting	pining	two hens

18. Going on a Major first date

In some situations, particularly Science and Humanities subjects, numbers are also important.

There is a peg system known as the Major system (also known as Herigone's Mnemonic System) to help, and although it takes a little while to grasp, it is incredibly clever.

It uses sounds and visual hooks to relate numbers to consonants in the alphabet. Each of them has been well thought through, although in researching this method, I found several deviations, so I would advise any teacher using this method to share their order and coding system with others, to avoid any errors.

Overleaf is the system, with some explanatory notes to help learn it more easily.

To use this system, you need to:
• convert the numbers needed for recall into letters; and,
• transform these letters into a memorable word or phrase.

Numbers and dates can be notoriously difficult to recall, yet for some subjects, they can be crucial in hooking understanding. Let's use the birth and death dates for Henry VIII to demonstrate this method.

Henry VIII was born in 1491, which using the Major system converts this to a range of letters.

Number	Letters	Notes
0	S Z X soft C	All relate to the z sound of *zero*
1	T D	Both letters have one vertical line in upper and lower case
2	N	Both upper and lower case N has two lines
3	M	Both upper and lower case M has three lines, and the letter looks like a sideways 3
4	R	The R is the final sound and letter of *four*
5	L	The Roman numeral for 5, and 5 fingers on your *Left* hand
6	Sh Ch soft G	The upper and lower case G look like a 6 rotated
7	K	Upper and lower case K look like two 7s
8	F V Ph	The cursive F has two loops, similar to an 8
9	P B	Lowercase P and B look like a rotated 9.

Remember, with this system, vowels and silent consonants such as

H and Y are left out intentionally, to act as fillers.

1	4	9	1
S Z X soft C	R	P B	S Z X soft C

Immediately, SRPS leaps out to me as S(C)RAPS - something Henry was famous for in his day. If you can conjure up the image of a baby like Henry VIII having lots of scraps with his Royal nannies, and know this system, his birthdate is able to be memorised more easily.

He died in 1547. This is coded below for ease of use.

1	5	4	7
S Z X soft C	L	R	K

Again, a word isn't too hard to identify horizontally - and CLRK is so close to CLERK as to be unavoidable. Imagine a Clerk to the Palace recording his death. Both dates now have an image, linked to a word, which encodes to a date.

19. I've got the key, I've got the secret

Keyword memorisation is likely to be more common than other techniques in the classroom, and is incredibly useful for helping to recall technical and foreign vocabulary, although its uses can cover every subject.

This technique of recall uses a bridge from a word to a meaning (or translation), using the key for the middle part. As an example, at Primary level, I've found that children often mix up the terms area and perimeter, interchanging them regularly. I needed to join one to a meaning.

PERIMETER - key - The distance around the edges of a shape

Looking at the word, you can see the word RIM in the middle. I used this as a keyword aid for the class. To make it instructionally clear, I held up a jar, and wound my finger around the RIM of it. As I did so, I talked about the perimeter of a shape.

- The rim of a jar goes all the way around the edge
- The perimeter of a shape goes all the way around the edge of the shape

In the example above, there was nothing particularly revolutionary or unusual about the image, but keywords often rely on strong visualisation - the more absurd and unusual, the better.

Languages benefit from keyword recall techniques since foreign words don't often have any attachment, so have to be learned by rote or using key words. Take learning the verb to buy in French, *acheter*. There is nothing about that word that looks or sounds like buy, sell, shop, purchase. Now imagine a French shop which just sold ashtrays. Say to yourself, "I went to the shop to buy an ashtray." The verb has been keyworded, and will already be quite 'sticky' in your mind.

The keyword method of memorisation, as with all memory techniques, is not without its costs however. If a student can't recall the key itself, then the word they have encoded with it is locked away too[53]. People tend to use this technique to remember details automatically; does placing it within the strictures of 'learning something educationally' (an admittedly ghastly phrase) change the process?

Certainly with technical and language vocabulary, it could be argued that the keyword method is biased toward *translating back* to an english word or understanding than the other way around. Seeing *acheter* might prompt someone to remember *ashtray* and link to *buy*, but nothing about the word buy makes a strong mental link to ashtray. With this in mind, the keyword method has certain flaws which are worth exploring within your own expertise.

[53] Crutcher, Robert J. "The role of mediation in knowledge acquisition and retention: Learning foreign vocabulary using the keyword method." Institution of Cognition Science University of Colorado, Boulder (1990).

One challenge to this is the perimeter example, which falls under Dual Coding theory[54]; it effectively works both ways, and thus is a more ideal (though less easy to identify or encode) form of keyword technique.

[54] Clark, James M, and Allan Paivio. "Dual coding theory and education." *Educational psychology review* 3.3 (1991): 149-210.

20. Memory Palaces

Known also as the Method of Loci ('places' in Latin) or Learning Walks, this utilises a familiarity with a physical location married to an unfamiliar set of information which is required in a particular order.

Dating back to Greek times, there is a famous story about a feast attended by Simonides, an orator, who was dismissed part way through his performance, but before a structural fault forced the building to collapse on the dinner guests, rendering them unrecognisable in the devastation which followed. Simonides recognised that he could recall who was there by picturing in his mind's eye who was sitting where around the table, and thus a fable was borne around the Method of Loci. No other memory technique has such a brilliant hook and dramatic backstory as this method, and it is used by many of the world's most successful memory competitors.

Its efficacy is also in no doubt[55] - this technique works incredibly effectively, with research showing that this method of memory particularly suited younger people, and that feedback increased recall gains.

---

[55] Rebok, George W, and Laurie J Balcerak. "Memory self-efficacy and performance differences in young and old adults: The effect of mnemonic training." *Developmental Psychology* 25.5 (1989): 714.

So how does this technique work? Recall, in detail, the journey from where you are reading this now to work (or if you are reading this at work, your journey home). Write down a list of unrelated items to recall, such as a shopping list, then at each point of this journey, place one of these items. It has been found that mental images need to be exaggerated, pronounced and absurd to be particularly effective, so don't imagine a small cooked chicken sitting on the roundabout; instead imagine a giant dancing raw chicken on the roundabout.

Once you have travelled on this journey, do it again in your mind, writing down the list. You will discover that the list can be recalled backward, forward or at any point in between. It sticks in a way trying to memorise a list conventionally wouldn't.

Abigail Mann, a Leading Teacher in a Hertfordshire Secondary, has used Learning Walks in her GCSE revision lessons.

She has found that they help the students recall the most important elements of their syllabus. Abigail takes the students on the journey itself around the school, describing each element in what she calls a "totally ridiculous story." The students are able to recall the lists for many months afterward, emphasising the retention rate of something married to both the mental imagery and physical location.

To get any lasting benefit from this technique, time in feedback needs to be spent looking at how it could be used in other learning scenarios, with students able to recognise how it can be used, and perhaps even *why* it works so well. As a tool used by many public speakers, it can have many untold benefits beyond memory competitions or GCSE revision classes.

21. Summary of Mnemonics

Clearly in day-to-day life, it would take an age to constantly encode, recall and decode vast quantities of information.

As is underlined throughout this book, techniques such as mnemonics are strategies to aid recall, but also are techniques the students can be encouraged to use if they were to revise information for an exam, to learn a key principle in a subject, or even as a methodology for a topic genre.

There is a clearly steep learning curve to these skills. At the outset, the load (effort) will be heavy, but the distributive benefits in the future, especially with regular prompts from the teacher, give this technique a genuine longevity.

Transferability of this skill is an essential part of long-term gain. If it is seen as analogous to only Geography skills, some students might not make the leap that it is in fact a highly transferable technique to draw upon for a variety of settings and uses. I prefer to speak publicly without notes, and have used Peg Words to learn a speech before, using each theme I wanted to, attached to numbers.

VISUAL THINKING

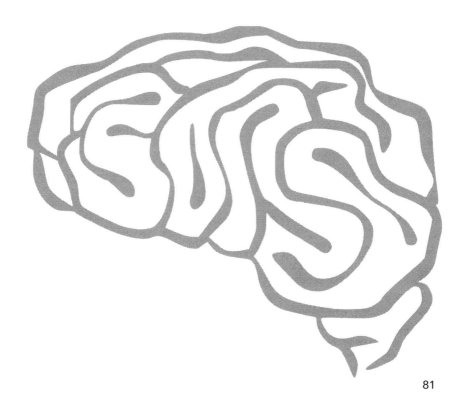

22. Picture this learning

Our world of pictorial instruction is pervasive. From road signs to LEGO instructions, the skill of transferring key information via a representative image is deceptively difficult and deserves its status as an artform.

What is perhaps less well recognised is how powerful using spatial and graphical representation can help with learning too. There is a common meme in Education that 'no-one remembers a good worksheet,' but I would argue that some of the best learning is threaded into everyday experience, and thus not that easy to explicitly recall.

Using LEGO instructions as an example, their sparse information has been pared down to the absolute essentials. In a quick analysis (for that, read 'flick through') of instructions, In found no words used beyond the front cover. In the ultimate test, you could perhaps give an indigenous tribe a pack of LEGO, instructions and have some hope that they'd be able to build a model with the minimum of help. Would they end up with a complete model? Yes. Would they recall the building process? Perhaps. Would they remember the diagrams used to help them in this task? I would suggest this was unlikely.

In the same way, giving spatial and graphic organisers to children may well help to scaffold their learning. While scaffolding is not uncommon in Education, where metacognition assists is in teaching these organising models explicitly, so that they might be drawn on in other learning opportunities. The end aim is for a student to be greeted with a challenge and for them to be able to mentally place an effective model to use against this challenge which will help them to succeed. What happens here is the removal of a scaffold (which to my mind is something teacher-constructed), replaced by something far more personalised in the form of a framework of understanding, adapted by the student according to need.

This section explores the use of such organisers, the research behind the benefits of them (with an Effect Size of 0.93[56]) and how they are successfully implemented in schools.

This section comes, as with most other sections in this book, with a caveat. Much of what is described here is what could be seen as teaching grandma to suck eggs. You could well be tempted to consider that you already teach this. Please read the following with an open mind, prompted by the key question:

"Do I use these or do I *teach the use* of these?"

It is hoped that by the end of this chapter, you will recognise the influence of your students' learning if these are taught for use, since it is a far larger jump for a student to adapt one learning technique to another learning environment than one might imagine.

---

[56] Scruggs, Thomas E et al. "Do special education interventions improve learning of secondary content? A meta-analysis." *Remedial and Special Education* 31.6 (2010): 437-449.

23. Space in any direction

The spatial organisation of information has been acknowledged by several (admittedly small-scale studies), which favour its ability to help retain factual information over linear information organisers.

When compared to text and outlines (data lists), spatial organisers have demonstrated more successful recall[57]. A spatial organiser is one where information has been shared in a format where it can be read in any direction. As an adjunct aid (that is, any study aid which isn't simply text), it enables students to compute relationships more quickly, and also requires less effort. Adjunct aids can include tables, graphs, concept maps, flow charts and visual diagrams of understanding; the very graphics which students use in helping their revision, turning pages of notes and text into quick-to-digest visual prompts.

This 'easier effort' goes against a common theory that learning requires a large amount of effort (also known as grit), but in this sense, it is where the effort is directed toward which makes the difference, as the following text and table hope to demonstrate.

When reading a text, it is suggested that the effort is directed into processing this information. With a spatial organiser however, the

---

[57] Robinson, Daniel H, Sheri L Robinson, and Andrew D Katayama. "When words are represented in memory like pictures: Evidence for spatial encoding of study materials." *Contemporary Educational Psychology* 24.1 (1999): 38-54.

effort is directed into encoding this information, with the student able to view relationships and discern patterns and trends more easily. Since our minds like to see relationships, this type of effort can be seen as less strenuous than reading and processing a text with the same information.

	Set text	Spatial organiser
Format	Prose	text and graphics
Retention	processed	encoded and processed
Relationship	indicated	suggested
Effort	high	low

It is hoped that the spatial organiser table above makes this point clearly; perhaps more clearly than the text preceding it. Some readers may even have skipped the text to read the chart, demonstrating its ease of access to a reader. It highlights the attractive factor of tables, graphs and diagrams, and to vandalise a common quotation, an organiser can speak a thousand words.

By summarising information in such a table, a teacher is producing two things. They are removing extraneous text (connectives and the like), and they are also 'breadcrumbing' the opportunities for students to form relationships between the information.

Clearly, the encoding is a complex skill which needs teaching, refining and developing, and the way a teacher helps a student to learn this is many and varied, including (but not limited to):

- Interrogation of the data
- Forming hypotheses
- Explaining connections and relationships
- Building a bigger picture
- Converting textual data into adjunct aids
- Completing cloze procedures on existing adjunct aids

Examining this list, how much of our time do we devote to these tasks with texts, which sometimes only require processing, compared to spatial organisers? As teachers, we can occasionally believe that economy of output represents economy of effort, but this is not the case when having to organise information in a non-textual format. "Writing a summary paragraph" is not perhaps an ideal vehicle if we are wanting students to retain information, let alone encode it for future access, and research on the way memory operates agrees.

The theory behind the success of using these aids is that information is stored in different forms in our brains. Textual information such as prose is stored verbally, whereas information presented as adjunct aids are stored both graphically and verbally, making them more accessible.

24. Using the graphical organiser as a template

Although scaffolding is assumed to be widely used, there is an inherent multi-faceted danger upon their reliance.

Scaffold models tend to be used in isolation, and it is suggested that they are teacher-led; that is, created by the teacher for the students, rather than in partnership with them. To extend the analogy of the term itself, one scaffold framework only operates successfully for the construction it is built around, so without any explicit direction over how the scaffolding is constructed, any transference to another topic or subject is serendipitous at best.

Secondly, using scaffolding can be accused of 'recipe learning;' that is, formulaic learning which the students build against, with little effort into knowing what the next step is they could make independently. This is the strongest charge against scaffolding; that thinking is lowered for the students.

Thirdly, scaffolding can be seen very much as a linear learning model. By its nature, any linear model relies upon the student completing each stage in sequential order. This of course works successfully when each stage is correct, but fails when one stage is incorrect, or a student does not know how to complete it (preventing them from progressing). If thinking skills are a process rather than a linear occurrence, it makes sense that the best graphical organisers don't always operate in a linear sense.

Certainly if you view many of the online resource banks for teachers, scaffolded learning appears to be incredibly popular, especially when compared to Teacher Books, which tend to instead have graded work and challenge rather than scaffolded tasks; a subtle difference. It would seem to suggest that scaffolding is seen as a lighter, simpler go-to for teachers in a rush. Good scaffolding needs thoughtful planning of its purpose.

Yet the benefits of scaffolding are numerous. One study of using a model for teaching problem solving in Maths reported a multitude of positive results, not least the confidence of teachers, which in this case increased from 50% confidence in teaching problem-solving, to 100% after the intervention[58], with 80% rating themselves as 'very confident.' This itself indicates a curious area worth exploring, especially with regard to the increase in results (detailed overleaf) - did they increase from using a an organiser, a more confident teacher, or a combination of both these factors?

In the study, student success rates grew by an average of 19%. When analysed further, the Effect Size was measured against three criteria:

	Effect Size
Mathematical knowledge	1.94
Strategic knowledge	1.16
Explanatory skills	1.51

---

[58] Zollman, Alan. *The Use of Graphic Organizers to Improve Student and Teachers Problem-Solving Skills and Abilities.* HTW Dresden, 2011.

While it should be emphasised that this was just one small-scale study, the Effect Size scores are fascinating, not least because the last core skill of explaining oneself scores so highly. It would appear to suggest that by using an organiser to help make sense of problems in a nonlinear fashion, it also contributes to a student's ability to explain themselves in a coherent, linear way. By emphasising the process rather than the scaffolding structure, students are able to better deliver that process back in their answers in a linear (in this case, paragraphed) format.

In other words, removing a linear instruction when teaching can help to deliver a linear response from a student. Graphical organisers are more powerful than they first may seem.

25. Goodbye text?

Does this mean that text should be phased out in favour of exclusively adjunct aids? Not at all - numerous studies have shown that the two combined give the greatest success with retention when measuring factual recall.

This occurs whether the text is read or heard. In short, the aid can help to understand and hook our interpretation of the text beyond simply having the text itself[59]. Why would we not use them then?

Take as an example the study of Shakespeare's Romeo and Juliet - perhaps his most famous play, in which the complex family relationships play an integral part of the plot and understanding the motivations of each member.

Below is a paragraph of the Capulet family, abridged from the Wikipedia entry, with traits and character detail removed.

Lord Capulet is the patriarch of the Capulet family, the father of Juliet, and uncle of Tybalt. Capulet's wife is the matriarch of the house of Capulet, and Juliet's mother. Juliet is the only daughter of Capulet, the patriarch of the Capulet family. Tybalt is Lady Capulet's nephew and Juliet's hot-headed cousin.

---

[59] Kulhavy, Raymond W, William A Stock, and William A Kealy. "How geographic maps increase recall of instructional text." *Educational Technology Research and Development* 41.4 (1993): 47-62.

It reads a little like the logic puzzles found in children's books, where you have to work out who is sitting next to who at a birthday party. Compare this with a family tree[60] of the Capulets (with all the supplementary family members added).

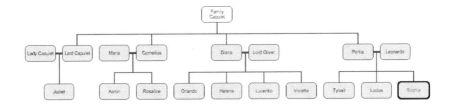

Which format of family information is more likely to be beneficial to students studying Romeo and Juliet? With the text, students would need to reread it several times when they required support in understanding the familial relationships, whereas the family tree model shows relationships in a format which can be read quickly, and which appear to require less effort to understand. As a scanning device, students can also get the information they want in a small glance, rather than having to read a different format of text for that information.

With this in mind, is it not a surprise that students use this format to help with revision? How often do teachers use these in combination with the text itself? In my book for Primary Lessons, I propose creating family trees with the students while a book is being read, thus supporting the text, as well as aiding the

---

[60] *Produced using the website www.familyecho.com*

understanding and encoding process of information contained within that text[61].

Consider the Roald Dahl range of books as an example of a way creating a family tree can help build up the picture of family dynamics - the full-to-bursting three generations of Charlie Bucket for example, all under one roof, or the simple and choking isolation of Danny, Champion of the World.

Creating a family tree can also be used for creative work, either to build a picture of a family for a proposed narrative, or to be given one with which to use as a creative muse for a story.

Alternately, a family tree diagram could be used for revision purposes, with students filling in gaps and writing notes around the different family members. The use of tracing paper could be productive at this point, to create a new level of emotional relationships between the different family members. I have used this method with eight-year-olds (although not with the *Romeo and Juliet* text admittedly) to great success.

---

[61] "100 Ideas for Primary Teachers: Outstanding Teaching" Stephen Lockyer, Bloomsbury, 2015

26. Enter the Matrix

Thoughts may appear linear in appearance, but they can often not be linear in terms of approach, validity or relevance. So how can you organise thinking?

By validating decisions, a second process to thinking occurs - positioning and justifying. Put this within a context, and you deepen thinking beyond simply recall. One excellent way of encouraging this process using graphical organisers is employing a matrix.

Here is a matrix for you to explore this method. Within the box are two axes, with the end points labelled. Place where each curriculum subject sits, aligned with the correct place on the matrix.

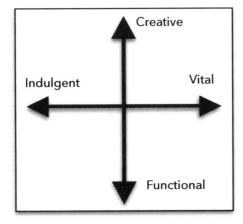

Although Primary-aged students are able to use this type of matrix, a simplified method of this thinking technique is to just use one axis, and have the students plot their answers on one scale. This could be extended to ask them to plot the same data points on the other axis, and see if they could combine them. I have found Year 4 able to use the matrix method with ease.

Using the matrix helps to emphasise sorting categories, as well as highlighting viewpoints and relationships between the data points - one might imagine an Art teacher placing their subject in the top right quadrant for example. This can lift information to a two-dimensional form, as well as depicting similarities and disparities. One study found it to be a particularly effective tool for solving problems[62], while another highlighted consistent effects in boosting relational learning[63].

In terms of 'compare and contrast' tasks, the matrix is quite a useful tool for forcing students to contextually justify their views on particular matters, and one in which debate and discussion can further embed considered opinions.

[62] Schwartz, SM. "Representation in deductive problem-solving: The matrix." 1972. <http://psycnet.apa.org/psycinfo/1973-08462-001>

[63] Kiewra, Kenneth A et al. "Supplementing floundering text with adjunct displays." *Instructional Science* 27.5 (1999): 373-401.

27. Story Maps

A common feature in working with narratives, the story map as a graphic organiser is a tool designed to make students distill their thinking about a story into a few salient points.

There are a multitude of story maps available for many age groups, from the most basic which covers Beginning, Middle, End (Set up, Conflict, Resolution) to much more in depth structures, where the story 'journey' can be unpicked and placed against generic categories. It is in using these categories that pupils are able to see relationships between stories, as these rarely differ too much when attached to a common framework.

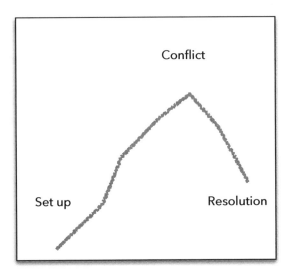

One such comparison found online is that of Star Wars to Harry Potter, where there are so many crossovers in the plot that Happy Potter seems to be a mystical remake of Star Wars. Indeed, the examination of these relational aspects leads to deeper understanding for the students[64].

This deeper understanding was brought to light to me after taking some advice from Helena Marsh, an Assistant Head who in her English lesson, used the famously-brief six word story (incorrectly attributed to Ernest Hemingway) to inspire similar reductionist plots. It read:

For sale, baby shoes, never worn.

This idea was utilised in my classroom but rebranded as six-word summaries. I found that students were able to think far more carefully about the story they had been studying when completing this seemingly-simple task. I further extended it to 20 and 50-word summaries. As one student was overheard saying to another, *"You've got to use Fox as one of your words if you're writing about 'Fantastic Mr. Fox'!"*

Story Maps can be used in two ways - as a reflective tool for a known story, or as a creation framework to help a story be generated. As with all graphic organisers, students need to be shown how to use them. In the story map case, the simplest way to encourage this is to allow them to scaffold an existing known story upon it, allowing the students to see the various elements at play.

[64] Gardill, M Cathleen, and Asha K Jitendra. "Advanced story map instruction effects on the reading comprehension of students with learning disabilities." *The Journal of Special Education* 33.1 (1999): 2-17.

Whilst they may be seen as good scaffold tools, I have only ever had mild success from them as a simple plotting device.

Their true benefit lies in deepening comprehension of a story in retrospect[65]. One effective way to use them is to to introduce the elements before a narrative, and highlighting the elements as the narrative leads to them. This way, the students are more familiar with the different ways they combine together cohesively.

Why these aren't used in other subjects and contexts often surprises me. The story of coastal erosion or the Break with Rome could be explained effectively using a Story Map, and would help students to see all the comprising parts, especially the point of conflict.

Taken further, even solving a Maths Problem follows the same points of a basic story map, and in making the narrative of a problem visible, may give students a better grasp of the individual elements of a problem, and indicate where they might be stuck.

---

[65] Boulineau, Tori et al. "Use of story-mapping to increase the story-grammar text comprehension of elementary students with learning disabilities." *Learning Disability Quarterly* 27.2 (2004): 105-121.

28. Semantic Maps

The much-favoured semantic map, or spider diagram as they may also be known, has several close counterparts. Although they may be seen as 'learning lite,' there is research which supports their use in improving comprehension, specifically in reading[66].

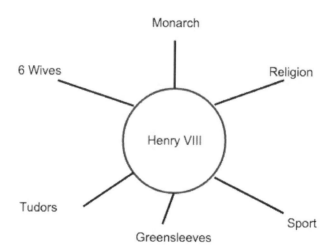

The humble spider diagram can be used in a multitude of ways, but based on a non-linear thought-process, these are

[66] Kim, Ae-Hwa et al. "Graphic Organizers and Their Effects on the Reading Comprehension of Students with LD A Synthesis of Research." *Journal of Learning Disabilities* 37.2 (2004): 105-118.

exceptionally good for assessing students' prior knowledge, as well as their gained knowledge after a topic or lesson. An adept teacher will be able to use both these to see the gains made, as hopefully there will be more new additions on the later version.

The semantic map has a poor reputation as it is quite an effective occupying task - students will often work industriously on a spider diagram, independently and for quite a sustained period. The danger is that this is simply a recall exercise - effectively a memory task. The thinking going on here is not especially deep or meaningful.
The way to improve spider diagrams beyond recall is to pimp them using specific devices.

Nested spider maps are spider maps with second and third order levels to them. If you were to ask students to start a map with Henry VIII at the centre, you might get themes around the outside, or stray facts. Nested maps require students to revisit each of these initial ideas, and expand on them as if they were separate spider maps. This gives a far deeper recall, and also encourages students to discern where they might put specific information, especially if the teacher asks them to validate their decisions. In the second round for example, would a student write about Queen Elizabeth connected to the category WIVES, MONARCHY, or both?

While there is an argument that technological tools[67] can help streamline the process of making spider diagrams, and in particular dragging the different elements around, technology can sometimes take the primary role over recall in this instance, which is why pen-and-paper methods of producing spider diagrams at this stage work better.

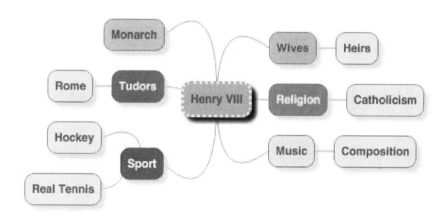

Mind Maps are another staggered continuation of the nested spider diagram, and again encourage the use of careful selection of category choice. A Mind Map is similar in look to a spider diagram, but with a judicious decision made by the teacher (normally) over the topics to be covered. This is best to occur with both the input of the curriculum and the input of the lessons (a

---

[67] *These spider diagrams were produced ion the website www.gliffy.com*

combination of both teacher and student input), leaving the students to fill the topics prescribed by the Mind Map[68].

Colour plays an important (although untested) role in Mind Maps for some teachers. Although this can 'prettify' the Map, careful thought should be made over the choice of colours used. Quite apart from considering any colour-blind children, a thoughtful teacher can select colours significant to the topics shown, both helping with recall for some, and reinforcing aspects of the topics themselves - using red for the Tudor thread and purple for religion in the example above for example.

[68] *The example was produced on the website www.mindmup.com*

29. And Venn I go and spoil it all

Created (or at least, named) by Mathematician John Venn in 1880, the Venn Diagram is able to categorise information into four distinct sets with ruthless efficiency.

Added to the delight of the Venn diagram is the ease in which it can be adopted and used by students of a very young age. I witnessed this first hand when observing a Reception teacher who took her class from introduction to understanding and using Venn diagrams in one lesson - the class were largely four-years-old at the time.

By using two overlapping circles, students are able to sift items and place them in one of four categories.

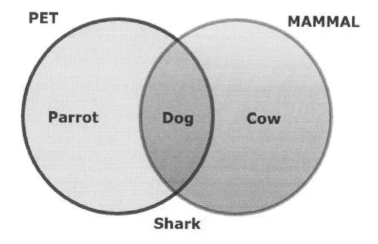

In the example overleaf, it should be clear to see that each of the animals fulfils the requirements of one of the sets indicated. Where their strength lies is in the ability to use comparison skills to consider where an item should be placed. While they are commonly used in schools, it is suggested that they are mostly used (a) in Maths, and (b) as cloze procedure tasks; that is, with only one right answers. This use is totally acceptable, but there are plenty of opportunities to use Venn diagrams in ways which encourage greater cognitive participation from the student. Consider the Venn diagram below:

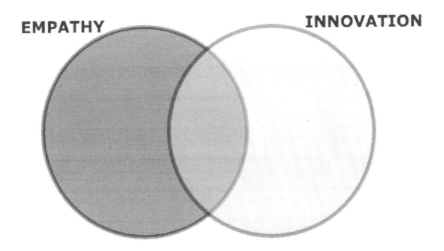

EMPATHY   **INNOVATION**

Consider the last five countries you have visited and place them in the diagram. How long will this take you because of the challenge of the question, and what sorts of logical reasoning will you have to consider to make an effective selection? Would a colleague or partner agree with you? Would you be able to robustly defend your choices?

Their simplicity disguises what is actually a powerful, critical analytical tool, which exemplifies the defining characteristics of using a graphic organiser according to Anderson-Inman and Horney[69], which are:

- To gain a non-linguistic holistic understanding
- Make thought and organisation processes visible
- Clarify complex thoughts
- Help to restructure ideas
- Promote recall and retention of information
- Assist with analysis

[69] Anderson-Inman, L. and M. Horney. 1997. 'Computer-based concept mapping: Enhancing literacy with tools for visual thinking'. Journal of Adolescent and Adult Literacy 40/4: 302–6.

30. Meaningful Mapping

Concept Maps take semantic maps a level further, forcing students to help organise and classify the relationships between elements on a semantic map.

These lines are usually labelled, and with a simple arrow (or arrows), can help to further explain relationships, as the example below indicates.

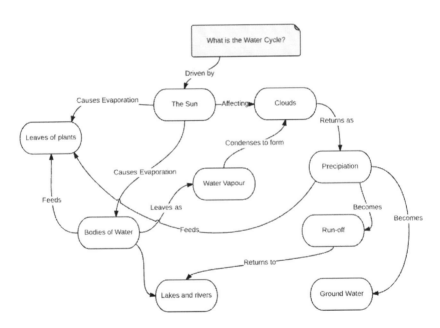

The indicating lines can perform three functions:

- Two-way arrow - both elements are connected
- one way arrow, to - "which affected x"
- one arrow, from - "which led to x"

The lines on concept maps are generally labelled, but this can be loose or in note form (including the use of symbols such as + or %). The two stages of labelling areas to join with an arrow include what the arrow is saying about the relationship between the two areas, and also what the arrow is labelled *as*. Once complete, teachers can use concept maps to view deeper understanding of the salient principles shared, but also identify misconceptions in understanding (both with the direction of the arrow, and how it has been labelled).

Concept Maps may also take several iterations to build[70], and have been found to be easier to follow and comprehend in a hierarchical structure, with the more important elements presented at the top.

For that reason, Concept Maps are perhaps one of the best tools for assessing the growth of knowledge gain over time. It would be interesting to see a student building a concept map over a course of lessons, viewing the growing interrelations between the elements and seeing which are the more significant elements which gain dominance in the diagram over the topic[71].

---

[70] *The Concept Map illustrating this section was produced using www.lucidchart.com*

[71] Indeed, any teacher who attempts this during a topic would be welcome to share their findings with me, for possible inclusion in a later edition of this book.

Some may view the essential element of learning as understanding the relationships between elements, rather than the elements themselves.

Even if a child knows that cold weather can produce snow and that water cooled produces ice, it takes the understanding of the relationship between these two facts to explain that snow is cooled water.

Not only is this relationship key, it is also much more transferable. Indeed, the earliest research into concept maps as a learning tool was focussed on supporting cognitive relationships within Science. As Novac et al. explained far more clearly:

"The fundamental idea in Ausubel's cognitive psychology is that learning takes place by the assimilation of new concepts and propositions into existing concept and propositional frameworks held by the learner[72]."

Creating these maps allows students to make the move from rote learning to meaningful learning, as defined by Ausubel[73], who defined meaningful learning as following three basic principles:

     i.   Clear and relatable material

---

[72] Novak, Joseph D, and Alberto J Cañas. "The theory underlying concept maps and how to construct and use them." (2008).

[73] Ausubel, David P, JD Novak, and H Hanesian. "Educational psychology: A cognitive view. New York, NY: Holt, Rinehart and Winston." *Culture, Cognition, and Literacy in Morocco* 285 (1968).

ii.   Relevant prior knowledge

iii.   The learner choosing to learn meaningfully

It should be clear that while the teacher is able to control the first two principles (by presenting relatable material and ensuring thorough prior knowledge), they can only indirectly affect the third. Indeed, many objective tests measure verbatim recall of knowledge, which can encourage a culture of explicit recall rather than meaningful knowledge (recognised by Hoffman in his book, "The Tyranny of Testing"[74]).

This is not to say that testing is inherently bad, or that recall is not a good basis for learning, rather that it is hard to make learning meaningful if teaching 'to the test,' as the current educational climate seems indirectly to encourage.

There is also the assumption that inquiry studies will assure meaningful learning, which of course is challenged by the third principle above. The researcher Novak argues that without conceptual understanding of the area they are studying, any activity may be little more than 'busy work.' This makes complete sense when considered; students may be able to recall specific information, but unless they are able to connect the information relevantly, the knowledge is simply recalled rather than meaningful. Although it appears that more GCSE questions encourage the relationship between facts to be an important area to test against, in Primary (ages 4-11), the emphasis is firmly on what you know, rather than what connects. This may seem to be irrelevant, until you consider that children as young as three are able to form meaningful connections. Is this a principle we explore

---

[74] Hoffmann, Banesh, and Jacques Barzun. The tyranny of testing. Courier Corporation, 2003.

enough in younger ages, or are we simply 'filling the jug' at this stage in Education?

It seems obvious, but making relationships between information can help to feed better recall. The human mind can typically recall 5-9 elements from a list of 12 unrelated facts. Make these relevant to the learner however, and this increases to around 10 items - for some, a two-fold increase. How powerful then is the formation of relationships, with them being able to double recall? Isn't it a wonder that this isn't more widely used in schools, since it would appear that the research suggests spending time building relationships between knowledge elements can help to not only make learning meaningful, but can also dramatically assist in the shallower end goal of helping students recall more.

Indeed, another advantage of meaningful learning is that it is embedded in memory much more deeply than rote learning, which is often learned for a specific purpose, and is quickly forgotten. I regularly have to repeat aloud six digit numbers sent via text from my Bank to authorise a payment - these are almost instantly forgotten, as they have no relevance or purpose to recall other than completing the task, and they disappear. Yet I am able to recall all the numbers of the houses that I have lived in, in order, because of their repetition, relevance and emotional connection over a long period of time. Research suggests that concept maps are relatable, as much as can be inferred given the knowledge of how our brains work, to the way we organise the information in our heads, both in a physical and psychological form[75].

[75] Bransford, John D, Ann L Brown, and Rodney R Cocking. *How people learn: Brain, mind, experience, and school.*. National Academy Press, 1999.

Shouldn't we model learning in the way our brains tend to operate most successfully, especially given that we know rote learning is so ephemeral?

There is also a cultural value given to the way work is presented. Judgements are made on the depth of learning when comparing a page of prose against a detailed concept map - certainly I would do this instinctively - despite a wealth of evidence against the contrary. Iconic memory is far more powerful and yet not understood as well; clinical tests found that recall of images had a success rate of 97% immediately after the test (in which subjects were shown 612 images in succession). Three days later, this figure was 92% and three months later it was an astounding 58%[76].

So how does one tackle the third principle, that of making meaningful learners? It is clear that some students find creating concept maps incredibly tricky. That is not to suggest that some types of learners find them inherently easier, rather than learners who struggle may well be more used to rote learning. Building relationships is a skill which needs to be *taught*.

Perhaps the best way to do this is to build a concept map alongside a project, with the students, so that they may observe and comment upon connections, and teachers can help feed this interest in a way that all students are able to start forming relationships between concepts meaningfully.

The poison of even deep rote learning is the misunderstanding of basic concepts, and relationships which are formed unchallenged

[76] Shepard, Roger N. "Recognition memory for words, sentences, and pictures." *Journal of verbal Learning and verbal Behavior* 6.1 (1967): 156-163.

due to a shallower explanation of these concepts. We all agree that getting closer to a fire will make you warmer; does being closer to the Sun indicate a Summer season? In an experiment, it was found that 23 out of 25 graduates could not effectively explain how seasons operate, missing out the key concept that the Earth rotates on an axis. Instead, they used the former explanation of 'closer to heat source' in many of their explanations, despite being a concept that they would invariably have come across several times in their education[77].

[77] Cabrera, D., and C. Colosi. "Thinking at every desk." Research Center for Thinking in Education: Ithaca, New York (2009).

31. Creating effective Concept Maps

Best practice in creating concept maps is to give them a clear context, with a focus question to drive a specific response.

In doing so, concepts are built up, and rather than these concepts simply being part of the focus, they are charged with being relatable. This stops students from simply listing concepts without any tangible connection, and encourages a growth in relationships between elements; in short, it forces students to explain relationships rather than list concepts.

Listing concepts is however a good start, as having done this, students can then weight the various concepts according to their importance (from essential to by-product), which helps to dictate the hierarchical structure of the concept map itself. It will also help to jettison any concepts which have been listed but which are unrelatable due to their irrelevance.

The eponymous Post-it note is incredibly useful in starting to make sense of concepts under a focus question, as their flexibility in placement allows students and teachers to move ideas around as the map takes shape. It is important to recognise that a concept map is subject to revision, as new information is imparted and new relationships become apparent. As this occurs, computer software such as CmapTool[78], or web-based solution LucidChart, can be employed.

The key advantage to computer software at this point is that concepts can remain and be moved, but that relationships also remain connected in a way that a drawn version would not allow without time-consuming redrawing.

One benefit in using the recommended tool is that it allows collaboration between students. Although this is possible in other ways (for example, using the drawing tools in a shared document on Google Drive, or the Collaborate feature on LucidChart), I have anecdotally found that the focus can be taken from building the map to using the tool itself, so it is seen as better to use a tool which focuses entirely on concept and relationship building, to better avoid distraction.

After the concept map is collated, cross-links should be sought. Two dangers occur at this stage; first, that sentences are used rather than concept words (since these could dictate the direction of a concept, rather than highlighting relationships). The other danger is that students create a 'string map.' where one concept leads to another in a linear fashion. A simple test is that of a prose translation - if the concept map can be turned easily into a sentence, it demonstrates only mono-linear relationships, and its value is diminished considerably in this context. This is especially common from committed rote learners, and can indicate poor comprehension. In this sense, comprehension could be taken to

---

[78] http://cmap.ihmc.us/

mean 'able to see and comment on the relationships between the elements.'

Creating the correct vocabulary to label the lines can be a source of frustration for some students. This is because it demands high cognitive functioning to complete successfully, so this is where both metacognition and grit come into play - it is this frustration, and overcoming it, that leads to stronger understanding for relational concepts.

My natural instinct at this point as a teacher would be to give the students a range of useful linking words, and while this may have a benefit for some students, there is an inherent danger in 'spoon-feeding' the scaffold. I am a firm believer in restriction or a blank canvas to enhance creativity, and as such, dialogue between students or between student and teacher is likely to develop far more secure terms, and better understanding of those relationship terms - most especially if they are in the student's own words. That is not to remove the importance of using key terms - but this is where secure prior knowledge of these terms comes into play. If a student isn't using a key relationship term, do they even know it or how to use it correctly?

In addition, the students forming their own relationship vocabulary helps as a powerful evaluation tool for the teacher, highlighting understood terms as much as misunderstood ones.

The element of collaboration in constructing a concept map cannot be overstated, as Prezner[79] concluded:

[79] Preszler, Ralph W. "Replacing lecture with peer-led workshops improves student learning." *CBE-Life Sciences Education* 8.3 (2009): 182-192.

"When students work cooperatively in groups and use concept maps to guide their learning, significantly greater learning occurs."

While there is justified angst in some educational quarters about the benefits of group work, this is primarily a behaviour and workload issue. What cannot be ignored is the growing body of work supporting greater cognitive benefits through working collaboratively. By using a computer program, teachers can remove elements of behaviour which can upset group work quite effectively.

Finally, these concept maps should be revised regularly and explored. Some students may benefit from using an omitive approach to concept maps when revising, and teachers may similarly present students with concept maps with either the concepts blanked out or the relationship terms hidden - both these techniques encourage students to explore relationships rather than simply knowledge recall.

32. Using Concept Maps for planning

While their use in helping to establish greater understanding for students should not by now be in much doubt, the benefit a concept map brings to planning a series of lessons can also be invaluable.

By using a specific question as an overarching aim for a unit of work, concept maps can be constructed by a teacher or team of teachers, and the resulting map (complete with cross-links) can help enormously in developing *what* to cover, and the skills needed. Using these as a form of planning preparation, and then sharing these with students, makes instruction 'conceptually transparent' to them, as Novac suggests[80]. As he says in his paper detailing research in using Concept maps,

"...students fail to construct powerful concept and propositional frameworks, leading them to see learning as a blur of myriad facts, dates, names, equations, or procedural rules to be memorized."

---

[80] Novak, Joseph D, and Alberto J Cañas. "The theory underlying concept maps and how to construct and use them." (2008).

By explaining how these elements are connected, and why they are being taught in this way, the learning moves from being a task of memorisation to one of better understanding and, for want of a better word, connectedness.

Making the concept map available, visible and accessible allows students to follow the key concepts, and I would be tempted as a teacher to go one further and make following this map explicit in the teaching. One might like to reveal elements as they proceed, or change the colouring of concepts and cross-links as they are covered by the curriculum.

Using a concept map for planning also allows a teacher to quickly identify gaps in either knowledge or understanding easily, and trace back errors in thinking, which should be easier to remedy. Whilst one method of using concept maps to evaluate learning might be to recreate either a partially-filled or blank concept map framework, it might also be worth considering setting a similar overarching question for students to answer using a concept map, and seeing which elements feature (and more importantly, which don't).

In addition, asking an expert in the field to recreate a concept map based on your initial enquiry question may bring up elements which you had not already considered as relevant or important. It takes a humble growing teacher to ask an expert for help, but can gain a multitude of benefits. The easiest way of doing this may be to ask online for help - experts are often keen to spread the word on their chosen subject, and you may well gain a visitor for the students as part of the exchange.

STUDY
THINKING

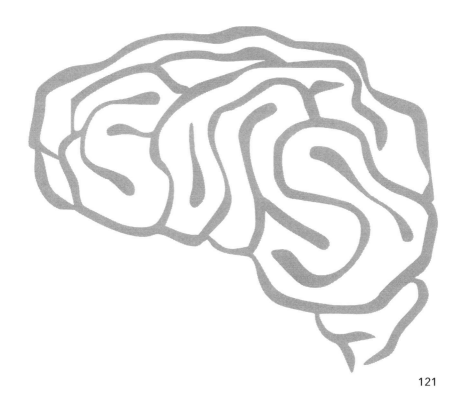

33. How we learn

This is an enormous question, and one that is outside the remit of this book. How then does metacognition help learning? By examining classroom learning strategies, and specifically teaching *how* we learn, we enable students to better approach the myriad of elements they are introduced to and review every day at school.

I recently spent a day at a conference. After a small keynote, there were five separate seminars, the last of which I was presenting in. Two seminal thoughts occurred to me both during and after this day. Firstly, I felt overwhelmed by the range of topics covered in the different seminars I attended. Although the overarching aim was to explore Research in Education, my head was spinning by mid-morning. I felt as though I had too much to think about already. It was then that I realised this was possibly a comparable experience for many of our students in school today, having to listen to a range of speakers and styles on a range of topics, and all demanding my full concentration.

Secondly, the knowledge I was to speak later clouded my thinking throughout the day. Although I was fully prepared, and felt confident that enough of my educational peers would be in the audience to remove many of my nerves, the knowledge I would have to present hovered above me. No wonder speakers dread the 'graveyard shift' of presentation (after lunch) when delegate brains are already full, and when nerves have wreaked havoc.

Again, I was able to relate this to a student experiencing anxiety over a forthcoming test, sports match or presentation they might have to give. What impact might it have on their learning?

The following section explores different learning strategies, and how we might actually teach these strategies beyond simply teaching the concepts of the curriculum. It may seem obvious, but in reality how often do we teach students how they learn? It was found that teaching learning strategies can have an Effect Size of 1.11, which is enormously powerful.

In addition, as with many of the metacognition techniques described in this book, the impact of learning these skills has the ability to pervade all future learning, potentially allowing this effect size to grow further. Techniques for learning are useful throughout adult life, so the impression is that these lessons can have reaches beyond simply achieving what is required to complete the latest unit of work in school. These strategies are so important, I advocate teaching them as soon as the teacher thinks possible, and perhaps even before that moment.

34. Strategy Instruction

Gaining an insight into the best method of learning information or how to solve a problem effectively can make the distinct difference between a good learner and a bad one.

Calling a student a bad learner can be seen as labelling the student unfairly, but knowing that there are more effective strategies which haven't been shared with the student actually puts the onus on the teacher to provide these strategies to the student, in order that they might fulfil learning in a way which makes the learning embedded when employed. To that end, explicitly teaching effective strategy instruction can reap enormous benefits.

Creating an effective strategy essentially means devising a strategy model which a student can employ across a range of disciplines rather than for one specific aim. The writer Polya published '*How to solve it*' in 1945, and it has been a popular book since then[81], explaining how to use the strategy model **Identify**, **Plan**, **Model** and **Check**. This small volume is also readily available online[82].

---

[81] Polya, George. How to Solve It: A New Aspect of Mathematical Method: A New Aspect of Mathematical Method. Princeton university press, 2014.

[82] "How to Solve It - G. Polya." Accessed 21 Sep. 2015 <https://notendur.hi.is/hei2/teaching/Polya_HowToSolveIt.pdf>

In it, he encourages the use of specific questioning from the teacher to get them to explore a problem from all angles. There is often a desire to leap into a problem before actually seeing what is specifically asked - although a question may be linear, solving the problem may require several interconnected steps and therefore be non-linear. He advises the following stages when trying to solve a problem, asking the same three questions for each stage; *where should I start, what should I do, what can I gain by doing so?*

- **Getting acquainted**: give yourself a moment to familiarise yourself with the problem
- **Working for better understanding**: identify the principle parts of the problem in turn
- **Hunting for the helpful idea**: with these principle parts separated, use prior knowledge to connect to these parts, considering how you have solved these problem sections in the past. Additional questions at this point include; what could I perceive, how can an idea be helpful, what can I do with an incomplete idea, what can I gain by doing so again.
- **Carrying out the plan**: break down solving the problem into steps. These may be big or small, but each should contribute toward the discovery of a solution.
- **Looking back**: After solving the problem, review your solution, how you came to solving it, and what lessons you learnt in the process of doing so.

Despite this method being over 70 years old, this is essentially the framework which Headteacher John Tomsett wrote about in 2015 while examining the use of metacognition in his school[83]. In his

---

[83] "This much I know about...The Sutton Trust/EEF Toolkit and ..." 2015. 21 Sep. 2015 <http://johntomsett.com/2015/02/13/this-much-i-know-about-the-golden-thread-from-evidence-to-student-outcomes/>

use of it, with claims of gains over just one lesson, the method he used was to have a teacher explicitly solve problems aloud, using a visualiser (which transfers what the teacher is writing or reading onto a screen the whole class can view) and near-constant dialogue of the teacher's thinking as they solve this problem. Although the stages aren't labelled as such, this is Polya's method made living.

Although there is a growing range of research into the benefits of using specific and systemic strategies for solving problems (cognitive strategies), the main element across all these strategies was that of metacognitive awareness [84] - put simply the student's awareness of the learning process they are following, knowing what is required to achieve good results in a specific task. Strategy models aid this process no end.

Of course, students tackle a range of challenges and problems even in their school time, and no isolated strategy can explicitly cover every eventuality. A robust strategy program would be one which introduces a range of approaches to address challenges, but also equip the student to make the right choice over the most preferential strategy to employ.

This is where the University of Kansas has built on its decades of research into learning strategies, packaging a program which details the many different models which may be used, into the SIM - the Strategic Instruction Model. It is a school-wide approach to teaching strategic thinking, entirely evidence-based, described in more detail in the next chapter.

[84] Campione, Joseph C, Ann L Brown, and Michael L Connell. "Metacognition: On the importance of understanding what you are doing." *The teaching and assessing of mathematical problem solving* 3 (1988): 93-114.

35. SIMulated Thinking

The *Strategic Instruction Model* from the University of Kansas has at its heart a range of approaches and components, developed from research carried out by the University, to aid any School or teacher wishing to improve their student's strategic thinking.

The core of the program is the *Learning Strategies Curriculum*, which utilises a range of skills spread over five themed areas. One such adaption of this curriculum can be found below[85], and is modelled on the Alachua County Public School curriculum. Those strategies italicised are described in further detail later on in this book.

The idea of an actual curriculum to cover learning skills may horrify some teachers and Senior Leaders. If we allow one half-hour lesson to cover the basics of each principle indicated below, this represents 13 hours at the very least to expose the students to the techniques - possibly the same amount of time a foundation subject might be allocated in one Primary School year.

Yet, if the research is robust enough to be trusted, this would be an enormous front-loaded investment. Statutory guidance for teaching hours in Key Stage 2 in the UK no longer exists, but a

---

[85] "Learning Strategies Curriculum Guide - SlideShare." 2015. 21 Sep. 2015 <http://www.slideshare.net/FAUZANBACHRIE/learning-strategies-curriculum-guide-elisa-wern>

recommended amount is 23.5 hours per week, equating to 846 hours[86]. Devoting 1.5% of this time to learning strategies would therefore require only the same percentage in gain to justify the running of the curriculum. Added to this, the amount of time given to each of these tasks in class normally would allow you to argue that the time given for a learning skills curriculum would be an

Theme	Strategies employed
Acquisition of knowledge	Paraphrasing, visual imagery, self-questioning, surveying techniques, SQ3R
Storage of knowledge	Guided notes, listening skills, Using symbols and abbreviations, verbal and visual word associations, identify similarities and differences, summarising and note-taking*, non-linguistic representation* (graphic organisers)
Expression and demonstratio n	Sentencing, test-taking, Jigsaw, generating and testing hypotheses*, cues and questions*, Cubing
Organising and Motivation Skills	Organising notebooks & backpacks, reinforcing effort and providing recognition, homework and practice*, setting objectives and providing feedback*
Social Skills	Cooperative learning, calming strategies, conflict resolution, comment consideration

[86] "Minimum teaching hours: EYFS, KS1 and KS2 – The Key." 2014. 22 Sep. 2015 <https://schoolleaders.thekeysupport.com/administration-and-management/structuring-school-day-year/recommended-teaching-time-per-week-for-key-stages-1-and-2>

enormous investment. To me, poor note-taking is akin to driving a car with hexagonal wheels; you may move forward but not with the smoothness and efficiency of circular wheels.

Take a look at the sample curriculum overleaf; how many of these principles do you expect the students to use regularly in their lessons? How many are also explicitly taught to those students, and how much in an inferred expectation from them?

Repeated use does not represent understanding, or acceptance that these are an effective learning strategy.

What is interesting about this curriculum model is the emphasis on cooperation and collegiality in the bottom section. Many of the strategies suggested in other categories rely upon a healthy working dynamic in the classroom, and this can be damaged by fractured working relationships. The asterixed skills are those mentioned by Marzano, highlighter further in this book.

One other incidental strategy indicated in the curriculum is organising backpacks. I would add to that tray tidies and pencil cases; thirty seconds of extra effort in locating items from a bag each day adds up to an hour and a half wasted each year; multiples of this are terrifying. One small strategy I employed in my classroom was to place a waste bin in each corner of the room and insisting upon enclosed sharpeners. It vastly reduced movement in the room and eliminated the 'sharpening circles' which are so common in Primary classrooms, in one fell swoop.

Clearly, this curriculum model was built around the needs of this School County in America, and a wise School would develop a Learning Skills Curriculum based around the needs of their pupils. This, combined with research on effective learning skills, and utilising the interests and abilities of their teachers, a bespoke curriculum would be incredibly powerful indeed. Sadly, this is unlikely to happen whilst we operate largely as silos in Education; perhaps we should employ the Jigsaw method to our teaching of these skills instead?

36. Don't be such a SQ3R

This is a reading method designed to improve a student's recall, by demanding five active engagements with the reading material.

Devised by Francis Robinson in his book 'Effective Study,'[87] it espouses active participation with a text rather than what students tend to do when reading for meaning, which is to read something twice. It employs surveying a text, also known as skimming or scanning; a methodology encouraged in the National Curriculum, but (anecdotally at least) rarely understood for its benefits.

The catchy name of this method[88] helps to recall the five methods required for this strategy, which are described overleaf.

Survey the text - Students are encouraged to read everything that isn't the body of the text; that is, the titles, sub-titles, chapter headings, blurb and reviews. This is to help formulate questions in the reader's mind which are hopefully answered within the body text itself. Although it may be misconstrued as such, skimming and scanning can often mean for the student *'read through the text really quickly and hope something leaps out.'* To my mind, skimming and scanning is akin to carrying out a one minute trolley dash through a supermarket, grabbing items at random, whereas surveying is the skill of stepping back and reading all the aisle

[87] Robinson, Francis Pleasant. "Effective study." (1970).

[88] I also like the way SQ3R looks a little like the word SQUARE; deliberate I'm sure, and it also ties in neatly with the mnemonic sections earlier in this book.

titles first, so that you might better comprehend the layout and positioning of the supermarket first.

Question - Formulate questions about the text. One suggestion for doing this is to convert paragraph headings into questions, or formulate questions based on what you want to find out in the body text, or what you might already know. Some advocates of this method encourage writing these questions down. An effective teacher might already hold up a text and ask questions about its content to the students, but the power of this model is in the students generating and asking questions themselves. Teachers obviously model this, but should also encourage question generation. Books with 'review' questions at the end of the chapter should have these considered too.

Read - This may seem trite but is a particular process which may also be more familiarly known as 'reading for meaning.' It employs the following steps; answering the questions generated before reading, rereading the captions to illustrations, reducing speed for difficult sections (note: the opposite of skimming and scanning), reading a section at a time, reciting after each section. Passive reading leads to the engagement a sub-par fictional book may give, where your mind is reading but not absorbing the material.

Recite/Recall - Either term is suitable, but the idea is the same; cover up the section you are studying and explain/summarise it to another person or yourself. This is an area where reading can be collaborative, but emphasis is placed on students using their own words to recite a section. One method of trialling this is to have reading pairs recall the text to each other, then separately write down their recollections.

Review - This is the stage of the strategy which really embeds what is written, and Robinson encouraged this to take place over the five days following the initial reading. After reciting the sections of text necessary, encourage students to write questions related to the areas they have highlighted in the main text. They should be encouraged to reacquaint themselves with the key points and be vocal in asking (and answering) the questions they noted beforehand, making flashcards for the questions they had some difficulty in answering. Use mnemonic devices, detailed earlier in this book, to help learn material needing to be memorised (note the stage at which this should occur). Students should then test themselves, reciting key information and creating their own study sheet or spatial map.

This method stands out as markedly different from the process of "read this quietly to yourself," which the students may be employing for want of a better and more effective method. Exposing them to this process reaches across far more than the subject they will learn this in alone.

37. It all fits together

The Jigsaw instructional strategy utilises each child in a group's ability to become an 'expert' within that group, and then teach others what they have discovered.

It is a highly cooperative learning strategy, built around the need for each member of a group to fulfil a specific role in order to distribute the focus. There are many teachers who are disparaging about group work, with those most critical who have correctly recognised that within even small groups, the weight of work tends to be borne by perhaps one or two members, the others passively coasting on their efforts.

By sharing the workload out, and assigning roles, everyone is able to become fully involved, and more importantly, the others in the group become reliant on each expert.

Made popular by Elliot Aronson in his 1978 book[89], 'The Jigsaw Classroom,' it has many variants, from different members of a group studying different topics, to the aforementioned 'expert roles' model.

The key aspect of an effective Jigsaw strategy is that everybody has to contribute. It relies upon the student's willingness to support their group by pulling their own weight, and so has a far

[89] "The Jigsaw Classroom." Accessed 22 Sep. 2015 <https://www.jigsaw.org/>

lower failure rate than simply splitting the students into groups of four and asking them to research the same topic.

When first introduced, the students will need plenty of guidance from the teacher. In order to make this strategy transferable (and in this case, I take this to mean that as a group they might decide the Jigsaw method would be best in research for example), these instructions need to be specific enough to enable the task to proceed, whilst the principles are exposed enough to be placed in another context.

One way to operate this is to ask students to carry out a specific area of study, then:

- As a group, introduce their names and roles in turn
- Each member shares what they have learnt
- Other members of the group listen, making notes
- The other members respond to the expert, echoing what they have learnt to dispel any misconceptions
- They then ask questions to clarify information or to open up new areas of research

While this method works well for research tasks, it has also been employed successfully in group reading activities, where roles are assigned, such as 'dictionary, summariser, reader, questioner.' Bill Lord, a Headteacher in the deepest Midlands, has employed this strategy successfully, transforming the way his Primary-aged students read more deeply as a group.

For Primary pupils, it may help to have the expert roles worn as badges or as Lanyards, so that everyone within the group is aware whose job is assigned to whom.

Secondary Teachers I spoke to who found group work successful described using methods which match Jigsaw, perhaps without realising. It was interesting to read the feedback provided by those Secondary teachers who don't support group work, as they often cite issues which Jigsaw methods seeks to address.

As adults, we are all expected to pitch in to group tasks equally, or at least, contribute what we would consider our fair share - yet this occurs more rarely than we might hope. One way to tackle this is to employ the Jigsaw method with adult groups - specific roles.

The other is to take retrospective measure indicators, which I have used with Year 5 upward. At a point in the task, you ask each group member to write down privately how much as a percentage they believe they are contributing. This almost never adds up to 100%, but does solidify an awareness that we all have strengths that the group as a whole should utilise. After all, if the task could be completed independently, what is the benefit of group work in the first place?

38. You Cube

The Cubing strategy is one which has grown in popularity, perhaps because the random nature it can take students adds an element of interest in an otherwise rather dry lesson.

It operates really simply; a blank cube has words, stimuli or questions on each face, and students roll the cube in order to deepen learning (it is intended).

The most common of this is to write the following on the six faces of a cube:

- Who
- What
- When
- Where
- Why
- How

Students have to roll the dice and ask a question of the text using one of these words at the beginning of their question to encourage a more diverse questioning range[90]. This can be extended further with 'deeper' words, such as:

- Compare
- Describe

---

[90] My book, "Hands Up: Questions to ignite thinking in the classroom" covers the power of questioning in more detail.

- Explain
- Contrast
- Dismiss
- Evaluate

While I have certain misgivings over adding random elements to a classroom, and fear that used inappropriately this could end up with students completing learning admin, there is an argument that this gives students an element of control in their lessons. It is also excellent for differentiation, as you can assign different coloured cubes for different differentiated groups.

There are a wide range of cube generators online should you wish to have printed cubes, and popular auction sites also sell dry-wipe cubes at a reasonable cost, enabling you to use your board pen.

I love dice in the classroom, and use them extensively, but have misgivings over the way that they can eat up precious learning time. To that end, I have found two solutions which work brilliantly.

The first is to contain all the dice separately in a small clear plastic container (IKEA offers enormous value for money). These contain the dice when shaken, stopping them from rolling over the desk or under tables and chairs, and reducing the distracting noise that dice are prone to make.

The other method is even simpler, and requires a little preparation and a paperclip for each student. In the case of the first word list, you simply add two more words into a 3 by 3 grid, leaving the central square blank. Students have a copy of this grid, and using a pen or pencil as the centre, spin a paper clip around this central point to randomly select a word to use.

This takes far less time than a dice, keeps the writing tool in the student's hand and can be used for a variety of purposes; I have used it mostly in Maths to generate random numbers for example.

who	what	why
how		where
which	does	when

A judicious teacher might create a page of these different grids and laminate them for repeated use. Alternatively, and in keeping with the concept behind this book, a teacher might also use these, modelling it effectively, and encourage students to employ it as a stimulation strategy in the future independently.

Cubes can also be used in fiction work. Consider the following list of topics which you might want students to explore further:

- Character
- Plot
- Twists
- Setting
- Conflict
- Resolution

Rolling a dice to encourage the focus of one element could be one way of engaging an otherwise uninterested student.

They can also be used to help generate fiction. After many years of yearning (coupled with a deep sense of frugality), I ended up buying a set of "Rory's Story Cubes"[91] after pressure from my eldest son. They are sickeningly simple - nine dice, each with a clear image on their faces. The idea is that you roll all nine and generate a story based around the nine revealed images. Here is a sample roll:

Mobile phone, magnet, book, clock, smiley face, masks, beetle, fountain, rainbow

For those children who need some form of mental stimulation, I can see these story cubes as being brilliant kickstarters. There is of course a whole range now, covering genres and story elements. There are 54 separate images - so in actuality it wouldn't take too long to create your own version[92].

Cubing Strategies can also work well with learning vocabulary - a dice with each face indicating a word to use in a definition or to explain to partner may well be less threatening than a dry list where a written definition is required.

---

[91] "Rory's Story Cubes." Accessed 22 Sep. 2015 <https://www.storycubes.com/>

[92] There is a lovely back story to the development of the story cube - Rory O'Connor originally put the 54 images on the coloured sections of a Rubik's Cube, and asked creativity delegates to mix up the sides, then choose a side (with 9 random images) to use as inspiration for a story. I love this use of a Rubik's Cube, and would be fascinated to see any use of this or any other teaching tool using this clever puzzle.

The creative teacher will no doubt come up with many more ways to use Cubing in their classroom.

39. Take note(s)

There are a multitude of note-taking strategies available online to look at and employ, but the Cornell method is one I most favour.

It utilises many of the techniques employed in the SQ3R Reading for Meaning system, but has distinct differences which enhance note making. The traditional note taking system is simply to note down or highlight salient points from a set text. This is beneficial for retrieval when looking at notes, but makes no major in-roads in understanding the notes. Added to this, the Cornell method helps not just with making notes from a set text, but also for talks, lectures and other teaching devices. It ends up being an excellent prompt for further study as much as a summation tool, and as such, really encourages thinking skills. A model note page is shown below.

Cue Column	Notetaking Column
...	
Summary Section	

Obviously, this table template should ideally cover an entire page. Devised by Walter Pauk in the 1950s when at Cornell University (and popularised in his book 'How to study in College'[93]), it follows a specific system, designed to encourage greater engagement with the source material.

Notes are made as they occur to the student in the right-hand column. Abbreviations and symbols are used, and key elements are paraphrased in a way which is quick and understandable.

As soon as possible after the note taking, questions are added into the Cue Column, which the notes tend to answer. This is good practice for exam technique, as well as reverse-engineering the learning. Subjects can be revised by covering up the right hand column and trying to answer questions from the left.

At around 24 hours after notetaking, a summary of the session is written in the bottom section, putting together all the key elements in one distinct section.

At each stage, students are required by the nature of the process to interact with the material presented: to summarise it, turn it into answers for questions they formulate and to reduce it into the key message. This is obviously far more beneficial than the swift 'highlight and run' technique which takes seconds to learn, but also allows the learning to last for mere seconds.

---

[93] Pauk, Walter, and Ross JQ Owens. *How to study in college*. Cengage Learning, 2013.

In addition, teachers who are given access to their student's notes can at a glance see the elements which the students deem to be most valuable for them to have noted down. The questions student place to the left may be used for examination tasks later, or to highlight areas of interest for future sessions.

One suggestion would be to download an Educational podcast from the many millions available online and trial this method. You won't look back on conventional note taking again.

Coming from a professor and with over 60 years of use, it is still wise to examine research conducted about this technique. This was carried out in 2007[94], and the researcher Keil Jacobs found that, when comparing Cornell Note taking to Guided Notes (explained below), there was a modest increase in scores when using Cornell Notes when compared to the Guided notes, but that students were able to answer more high-order questions. He concluded that Cornell notes are most successfully employed when asking students to synthesise information effectively.

Guided Notes are effectively 'fill in the blanks' crib sheets, produced by the teacher or lecturer, and scored much more highly in Jacobs' research, where the students were tested largely on recall. Guided notes lead a student through the material, often by leaving gaps to complete, or answering small questions.

Perhaps the best solution in an examination system which expects both recall and thinking would be to combine these two elements together, as this would benefit both the student and the teacher.

---

[94] Jacobs, Keil. "A comparison of two note taking methods in a secondary English classroom." (2008).

40. Marzano's Instructional Strategies

The *Learning Strategies Curriculum* outlined earlier in this book made reference to Marzano's Instructional Strategies - nine high-yield strategies which were were identified from a meta-research study covering over 100 research papers[95].

This book covers many of these nine strategies elsewhere in more detail. The Effect Sizes stated are taken from Marzano's book and calculations.

Setting Objectives and Providing Feedback

Giving students a clear direction for their learning and constant, relevant feedback in how well they are performing to their agreed learning objective has clear and beneficial gains. (ES 0.61)

Reinforcing Effort and Providing Recognition

Building connections between effort and achievement in the student's mind are crucial in improving their beliefs about learning. Recognition of effort and accomplishments related to this goal help to motivate students. (ES 0.80)

---

[95] Marzano, Robert J, Debra Pickering, and Jane E Pollock. *Classroom instruction that works: Research-based strategies for increasing student achievement*. Ascd, 2001.

Cooperative Learning

Opportunities to allow students to interact with each other in ways that enhance their learning are important and realistic. (ES 0.73)

Cues, Questions, and Advance Organisers

Helping students to organise their thinking and learning gives them greater extrinsic access to work, as well as feeding their understanding in the most fitting way to learn. (ES 0.59)

Nonlinguistic Representations

Utilising graphic images allows students to 'add to' their knowledge bases in ways which might be more accessible than simply text alone. (ES 0.75)

Summarising and Note Taking

The ability to reduce information down effectively not only enables deeper embedding through this process, but can also allow easier access on the main ideas captured. (ES 1.00)

Assigning Homework and Providing Practice

Giving work which allows students to practice review and apply knowledge gained can help their ability to achieve their expected levels of achievement or proficiency. (ES 0.77)

Identifying Similarities and Differences

The simple act of comparison can reap enormous benefits in terms of improving mental processes, as this engages student's subject knowledge in identifying similarities and differences. (ES 1.61)

Generating and Testing Hypotheses

Encouraging opportunities for students to use mental processes that involve making and testing hypotheses improves their understanding as well as their ability to use knowledge. (ES 0.61)

41. What's the SCORE with cooperative learning?

One popular Educational meme for group work features the four leads in the motion picture "The Hangover," with them labelled according to their role both in the film and in group work:

- The one who does 99% of the work
- The one who has no idea what's going on the whole time
- The one who says he's going to help but he's not
- The one who disappears at the very beginning and doesn't show up again until the very end

These will be very familiar categories for many of us. Students may well be willing learners, but unless they have the social skills which enable them to work with others, group work will be a wasted task and a lost opportunity.

The SCORE Skills program aims to address this fundamental need for a more cohesive working dynamic, and was developed by Webb et al.[96] as part of their SIM program. In it, students are explicitly taught how to:

- Share ideas
- Compliment others
- Offer help or encouragement

---

[96] Webb, Barbara J., et al. "Effects of social skill instruction for high-functioning adolescents with autism spectrum disorders." *Focus on Autism and Other Developmental Disabilities* 19.1 (2004): 53-62.

- Recommend changes nicely
- Exercise self-control

These all seem like good social skills which one would hope students already have, but this is clearly not the case. In studies carried out by the University of Kansas[97], students who were explicitly taught these skills improved from 25% in cooperative skills to 78%, an enormous leap. This, compared to the control group who moved from 25% to 28% over the same length of time, underlines how valuable these social skills can be in improving class dynamics.

The difficulty with social skills is that they may be modelled, expected or hoped for, but rarely are they actually taught to students in a program like this. Marrying the benefits of cooperative work with the opportunities for this type of learning make for a strong argument that students need guidance, training and feedback in sociability learning skills if there is to be any gain. Simply to say that group work doesn't work denies students the opportunity not only to become better learners, but in a long-term viewpoint, better citizens too.

Some school PSE (Personal and Social Education) programmes specify some of these socialisation skills, but I would argue that these are sociability-driven aims rather than learning-driven, and that there can be a strong disconnect between these two worlds in the mind of the student (and perhaps of the teacher or school too). Giving training in cooperative skills under the umbrella of learning explicitly equips students with an understanding that it is this dynamic that a group can work most effectively. More

---

[97] I have been unable to verify these results at the time of printing.

generally cooperative students as a result of this are a fantastic byproduct.

SELF-THINKING

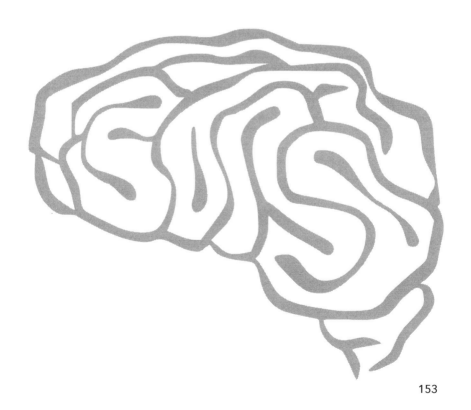

42. On your own two feet

Giving all these learning strategies to students is one thing, but enabling them to adopt and adapt them to their own learning needs is when their true power is apparent in the research.

To use a cooking analogy, we can make pancakes with a chef, or they can show us how to make them ourselves. It takes our own willingness to consider and apply what we have learnt in this process to transfer it to other cooking opportunities which beings external benefits.

One way in which this can occur is in *Self-Regulation Strategy Development*, or SRSD for short, which was devised and pioneered by Steve Graham and Karen Harris in their meta analysis of research into this work[98]. Although their research focussed mainly on students with learning difficulties, and particularly within the context of writing, what they identified was far-reaching; it is effective for all students and all learning.

They recognised, as many teachers will, that students appear to have a finite capacity for writing effort, and this can tail off quickly, especially when they are expected to generate creative work. The research broke down the most successful model for utilising a strategy, both to teach it, and for students to adopt. These stages are:

---

[98] Graham, Steve, and Karen R Harris. "Students with learning disabilities and the process of writing: A meta-analysis of SRSD studies." (2003).

- Develop and activate background knowledge (Class)
- Discuss the strategy, including benefits and expectations (Class)
- Model the strategy (Teacher)
- Memorise the strategy (Student)
- Collaboratively support the strategy (Class & teacher)
- Use the strategy independently (Student)

Note how the student is involved in all stages of the process, either listening and observing or actively contributing, whereas the teacher steps away in the latter stages of independence. It follows the "tight then loose" model of teaching, where the learning reins are passed to the student, to use a hamfisted analogy.

This model of strategy-building has itself a model for the students to follow:
- Goal setting
- Self-instruction (eg talking aloud)
- Self-monitoring
- Self-reinforcement

By training students to use this model on their own, you are encouraging self-regulation, and again, these strategies are transferable. What we are trying to develop are strategic learners, summarised by Vanderbilt University[99] as exhibiting the following characteristics. Strategic Learners:
- Are able to analyse a problem and develop a plan
- Are able to organise multiple goals and switch flexibly from simple to more complicated goals

[99] "IRIS | Page 1: Understanding and Using Strategies." 2015. 24 Sep. 2015 <http://iris.peabody.vanderbilt.edu/module/srs/cresource/q1/p01/>

- Access their background knowledge and apply it to novel tasks
- Develop new organisational or procedural strategies as the task becomes more complex
- Use effective self-regulated strategies while completing a task
- Attribute high grades to their hard work and good study habits
- Review the task-oriented-goals and determine whether they have been met

By contrast, non-strategic learners:
- Are unorganised, impulsive, unaware of where to begin an assignment
- Are unaware of possible steps to break the problem into a manageable task, possibly due to the magnitude of the task
- Exhibit problems with memory
- Unable to focus on a task
- Lack persistence
- Experience feelings of frustration, failure, or anxiety
- Attribute failure to uncontrollable factors (e.g., luck, teacher's instructional style)

These features are hopefully recognisable in the students at school, from both groups. The latter approach each task as if they are jumping out of an aeroplane without a parachute. We may even subconsciously blame their organisation skills or strategies, but without offering them any strategies to employ independently. I have certainly been guilty of this in the past, and can readily recall students who either are able to plough ahead in work without any structure, or appear trapped at the first hurdle, seemingly caught by having Fear of the blank page.

I discussed this with a teaching colleague, and we likened it to the two types of toy car my son plays with at home. The first is a free-wheeling type, where it needs the child playing with it to provide propulsion. The second type of car is one where you pull it back to 'charge' the spring, so when you let it go, it is self-propelling. We discussed at length how we could make our students more self-propelling, so that they were able to start a task (or at least, know what to do in order to complete a task) without the constant nudging of a teacher. The secret lies in giving students strategies to employ.

Let's look at the SRSD model in stages, using Newspaper writing as a working example.

Develop and activate background knowledge

Students would need to be exposed to different types of newspaper writing, and recognise he features which overarch this genre. There are likely to be areas and terms which the students are familiar with at this stage, so these should be clarified for understanding. Compare and contrast tasks are also useful at this stage, as they highlight both similarities and differences to guide the student.

Discuss the strategy, including benefits and expectations

This a vital stage of the process; students should be able to (by the end) recognise the strategy, how it will help them and what a completed piece of work should look like against this strategy. It is likely to have been formulated in the earlier 'background knowledge' stage; creating it at this stage is likely to further embed links for the students too. This is Extreme Scaffolding[100] made explicit for the students.

---

[100] Also a possible Channel 5 series.

What can help here is the use of goal-setting with the students, as well as the various ways that this strategy can be transferred to other journalism genres such as writing online or newsletter copy for example. Isolating the strategy leaves it very domain-specific, and thus weakens its impact overall.

Students can be given guidance to build their own goals for achievement in using this strategy, and the teacher should give advice for helping the students to track their own performance against these goals. In this task, it could be that another student in another class could read the text and identify what writing genre it belongs to, though not why.

Model the strategy

In our keenness for students to complete work, we can neglect this stage. The teacher proves the efficacy of the strategy by modelling it for the students. This is a stage which is often neglected, or at least, skipped hurriedly over, by teachers, but actively demonstrates the strategy in action. It also provides students with a model to look back on, and see the way that the example matches the strategy. By modelling the strategy with the students' involvement, they are also able to see clearly the link between the strategy and output.

One key aspect of this stage is not only to model the strategy, but also to model aloud the thinking processes the teacher is going through. This can be carried out by the teacher talking through the stages in the process they are going through, asking themselves questions, and regular checking that they are working against the criteria they have specified. They can highlight other supplementary tasks such as checking they are working toward their goal or checking their work at the same time. This 'talking thinking aloud' procedure really helps the students to understand

159

the thought processes occurring to the teacher. We can as a profession sometimes be guilty of giving an explanation automatically, cutting out the thought processes which occur simultaneously, when this is perhaps the most important aspect of this stage.

Memorise the strategy

While we might normally keep the various stages of the strategy, it helps to embed the individual elements by encouraging memorisation, so that students can employ 'hands free' thinking in their work. Earlier chapters on memorisation techniques can help with this, especially the Method of Loci.

The aim of memorising this strategy is that students won't have their flow interrupted by having to 'stop and think' - it would ideally be automatic (or as close to automatic as is possible).

Support the strategy

This is the stage which the teachers handhold the learning process with the students, and is possibly the most intense interactive aspect of the lesson. The teacher and student work collaboratively together on the work, using strategy charts and guidance (where necessary) to help them. The teacher will ensure they are aware of their goals (use more exciting verbs, ensure punctuation has variety), and are working toward them. Constructive feedback and positive reinforcement of both achievement and effort can be used with the students at this stage, but support can of course be modulated to those who need most guidance. The teacher should also ensure students haven't veered from the strategy in place, and guide them back on course if this is needed.

The ultimate aim is fluidity with the strategy, so that the students both have ownership of it, and can use it comfortably.

Independently use the strategy

This is not just the 'Big Write' at the end (which I feel gives undue emphasis on end products rather than the underlying process beforehand), but also in similar tasks which could also employ the same strategy. Students might miss out or adjust certain steps in the strategy, which gives the teacher further areas to develop with the students.

Further guidance, including an online training session on using the SRSD technique, is available free of charge on the Internet[101].

---

[101] The IRIS Center for Training Enhancements. (2008). *SRSD: Using learning strategies to enhance student learning.* from http://iris.peabody.vanderbilt.edu/module/srs/

43. The Direct Line to instruction

Education is one of sometimes polaric challenge, and *Direct Instruction* is one such Educational behemoth, seen both as the antithesis of any form of personality for our profession whilst extensive research identifies it as one of the most successful forms of teaching.

Put simply, Direct Instruction teaching is a strategy which uses (at its most extreme version) highly specific and sometimes scripted lesson plans, with no interaction between students, and very deliverable, functional worksheets. It is something I am enormously resistant to personally, despite the weight of evidence for its effectiveness, as I view it as lessons my Mum could teach (she, incidentally, is a retired Midwife). To me, you can teach but not be a teacher, where in this sense a teacher has an all-encompassing role as a guide, supporter, adviser and even sage.

Yet the research disagrees. Hattie's meta analysis found Direct Instruction to have an Effect Size of 0.81, which is remarkable, not least because of the disparity it has against those elements surrounding it in his list of most impactful interventions.

It is also the most common model, albeit diluted, of teaching, and follows the following stages:
- Introduction/Review
- Development
- Guided Practice

- Closure
- Independent Practice
- Evaluation

If you have read the previous section on SRSD, you cannot fail to see how similar these are with each other. Below is a breakdown of each stage, followed by a comparison of Direct Instruction against SRSD.

Introduction/Review

The teacher introduces the unit of work through a stimulus and explicitly sets out the goal of the work, sometimes called the learning intention. This could be related to what is more commonly known as the lesson starter. There are however three main types of starter that I've observed; one which 'warms up' the children in a subject-led but possibly context-free nature; one that summarises previous learning, and one that introduces the new topic. With Direct Instruction, it is a blended combination of the last two, with an important principle being the connection between these two elements.

Development

The teacher then models the knowledge or skill behaviours that students would be expected to demonstrate by the end, helping the students to process this information successfully and will not progress until they are assured of the students' understanding. This is our 'sage on the stage' section; what might classically called direct teaching. The term modelling is crucial here, as students can distinguish clearly between modelling and demonstration.

Guided Practice

Students would then demonstrate, with support from the teacher, their mastery of the work through tasks or activities. At this stage, the teacher would closely monitor student work, intervening where necessary.

Closure

At this stage, the teacher would recap what has been covered, and ensure that the goals for instruction had been achieved. Here is our traditional Plenary activity, using a form of assessment to ensure all students had shown progression from their starting point at the beginning of the lesson.

Independent Practice

This stage allows students to demonstrate their understanding of the learning through independent work - that is, work without assistance. Homework would of course be a perfect vehicle for this.

Evaluation

At this stage, the teacher would assess the student's understanding of the material, either through an end of unit test, assessment of their work throughout the work itself, or a combination of both these assessment strategies. They would then assign new goals for the student, based on this evaluation.

This could be seen as a traditional four part lesson, with homework and assessment sections added at the end. Certainly, this model seems to template most successful lessons. While it is successful for learning, it carries none of the transferability weight which SRSD has, in that it is an effective discrete learning tool. But are these two teaching strategies more similar than one first thinks? Certainly, Lee Swanson thinks so, and his research on them considers this to be the case[102].

He concludes that they are similar in two distinct ways; firstly that they share an agreement about effective methods of instruction (review, statements of instructional objectives, teacher presentation, guided then independent practice and formative evaluations of learning), and secondly at they follow a sequence of events. Swanson's meta analysis identified 20 common components of these strategies, which were:

- Sequencing
- Drill-repetition and practice-review
- Anticipatory or preparatory responses
- Structured verbal teacher-student interaction
- Individualisation
- Novelty
- Strategy modelling and attribution training
- Probing-reinforcement
- Non-teacher instruction
- Segmentation
- Advanced organisers
- Direct response/questioning
- One-to-one instruction
- Control difficulty
- Technology
- Elaboration
- Modelling of steps by the teacher
- Group instruction

[102] Swanson, H Lee. "Instructional components that predict treatment outcomes for students with learning disabilities: Support for a combined strategy and direct instruction model." *Learning Disabilities Research & Practice* 14.3 (1999): 129-140.

- Supplement to teacher involvement besides peers
- Strategy cues

Averaging the Effect Sizes across all 180 studies filtered for this research calculated an Effect Size of 0.79. What is interesting with this study is the research which combined both Direct Instruction and Self-Regulation Strategy Direction, which had an Effect Size of 0.84. He notes with caution that no isolated strategy can have such a gain; rather it is a combination of the most successful of nine from his 20 key components which make the most substantial difference. These are:

- Sequencing - breaking down learning into short activities or using step-by-step prompts.
- Drill-repetition - daily testing of the skills taught
- Segmentation - breaking down tasks into units that combine to make a whole, and modelling this process
- Directed questioning and responses - asking process-related and content-related questions, including entering into dialogue with students
- Control difficulty - sequencing the task form easy to hard, and only giving prompts where necessary
- Technology - Using a computer to create flow charts and so on to facilitate presentation
- Group instruction
- Teacher supplement - including homework, parents or other adults
- Strategy cues - reminders to use strategies and the teacher verbalising problem solving

Of these, 'Control difficulty' is highlighted as being the most effective single component, and is recognised as being scaffolded learning. Note that this isn't differentiation in the traditional sense, in that all students are taken through this scaffolding component.

How many of these components feature in your most successful lessons? Where could you add them, and what impact could they have if you did?

None of the components dealt with the concept of self-goals, which is another area of self-regulation and metacognition which is often misappropriated by teachers (not intentionally I believe), since there is a top-down focus on goals, often labelled 'targets,' drawn from the curriculum, rather than bottom-up built, created from need. Self-goals could perhaps be the most powerful tool in the cognitive learning arsenal.

44. Self-regulation

Zimmerman[103] describes self-regulation as students developing into "*masters of their own learning*," and it is becoming well recognised that successful students often have the attributes of a self-regulating learner.

They plan their work, set themselves goals, are organised, self-monitor rather than rely on teacher feedback or intervention (not that this isn't vital) and self-evaluate during their tasks. Importantly, they don't 'choke' when something unknown appears or one source of information appears to be unreliable.

These are all qualities we as teachers admire in students, yet it would seem that little time is spent actually teaching these skills (and they are skills rather than inherent traits). Self-regulation could be mistaken for independence by some, but there is a distinct difference. The self-regulated student is operating almost entirely on a self-evaluative quest against fixed standards, whereas the independent learner doesn't utilise the same mental self-checks to assure them that they are remaining on course. It is akin to a trained skier and an off-piste skier - both have skillsets which are admired, yet only one is sticking to the marked path.

---

103 Zimmerman, Barry J. "Self-regulated learning and academic achievement: An overview." *Educational psychologist* 25.1 (1990): 3-17.

Another feature of the self-regulated learner is that of a "self-oriented feedback" loop[104]. This is the internal process of constantly checking their learning effectiveness and progress, rather than waiting for an externality to change this. As a Primary teacher, I am faced daily with children who doubt the learning path they are on, regularly asking, "is this right?" almost ritualistically to tasks. The path to self-regulation for these children would be:

- Internalise this question
- Evaluate performance against understood aims
- Alter performance accordingly to a more appropriate format

This is what a self-regulating student does in the aforementioned feedback loop. They constantly question whether what they is doing not is right, but if it is on the right path. One favoured self-motivation cliche I particularly like is "a passenger aeroplane is off course for roughly 90% of its journey" - knowing the goal, and knowing you are working toward (if not directly) these goals, is a central feature of the self-regulated learner.

Another feature of the self-regulating learner is that, for them, learning and motivation are intertwined with each other; they proactively seek out opportunities to learn. Dream students! There is little more rewarding than a student, enthused by your lesson, racing up to you later in the corridor with further questions or thoughts; self-regulation in action.

---

[104] *Lasane, Terell P., and James M. Jones. "Temporal orientation and academic goal-setting: The mediating properties of a motivational self." Journal of Social Behavior and Personality 14.1 (1999): 31.*

I have witnessed this in my own children, whose drive to learn more about the game Minecraft has had them devouring tutorials, forums and videos in order to improve. Recent research has found that some children are reading graduate-level literature in order to stretch their learning[105].

So how can we get this Minecraft effect in all our students? Firstly, successful self-regulation is a combination of learning strategies, their responsiveness to self-oriented feedback and lastly the motivation to learn. It is because of this triumvirate that self-regulation is so hard to successfully teach - motivation comes from the student; we can feed this but cannot create or force it.

The methods which students themselves recognised as motivating them were researched[106] and included; self-evaluation, organisation, goal setting and planning, information seeking, record keeping, self-monitoring, environmental structuring, giving self-consequences, rehearsing and memorising, seeking social assistance and reviewing of text and notes.

It seems clear that if we are to feed motivation, teaching the students in our care how to best implement these methods in their school and home work lives.

What is interesting about this list of strategies is that it can also be used as a predictor for academic achievement. Depending upon the range and weighting of these strategies, researchers were

---

[105] Rowsell, Jennifer. "Toward a phenomenology of contemporary reading." *Australian Journal of Language and Literacy* 37.2 (2014): 117.

[106] Zimmerman, Barry J. "Becoming a self-regulated learner: Which are the key subprocesses?." Contemporary educational psychology 11.4 (1986): 307-313.

able to predict academic achievement to a 93% success rate[107]. If schools are looking for a panacea to exam accomplishment, successful self-regulation skills could be the solution they are looking for.

That these skills become inherent and life-long is in little doubt, but to assure yourself, consider the most successfully-academic adult you know - how many of these methods could you conceivably consider them using in their work life?

The answer for most readers would be many, if not all. Certainly when viewed personally, my success in work depends upon some of these factors being aligned to my ideal - I find it much harder to work in an environment where I don't have an upright chair and desk to type onto for example, whereas for others, they might find they can work in most environments.

What was an interesting byproduct of the research into academic achievement was the strategies used by lower-achieving students, which often focussed on externalities, or generalist statements such as using will power or working harder. If we use these terms in class, do we know what we mean by them? More importantly, do our students? "Clear away the crockery in your room" is likely to have more effect than "tidy your room;" clarity is essential.

Taking this investigation further still, the researchers asked teachers to score students on these methods, and found an 80%

---

[107] Zimmerman, Barry J, and Manuel Martinez Pons. "Development of a structured interview for assessing student use of self-regulated learning strategies." *American educational research journal* 23.4 (1986): 614-628.

correlation. Not only are teachers able to predict academic success based only upon their perceptions of how students self-regulate, but student perceptions of self-regulation are even more accurate.

It is not possible to simply teach students these strategies, however ideal or convenient this may seem[108]. Part of the difficulty is that it is hard for students (let alone teachers) to monitor the effectiveness of a particular strategy over another. It ends up being the judicious choice of the student to choose the best strategy based on their personal choice rather than its effectiveness over another one. Choosing the best strategy requires directed attention and sophisticated reasoning processes, both of which are skills that also need tailored teaching and time to develop. Research did however find that self-regulation training helped with students' learning and also improved their perceptions of efficacy[109].

Age does have an influence on self-regulation. Perhaps unsurprisingly, younger children are (on the whole) over optimistic about their ability to learn, have a vague understanding of academic tasks and their strategic knowledge is intuitive. In addition, they rarely reflect on their own performance, and believe that success comes from simply trying hard. This changes as they get older, with Secondary children in particular recognising that effort *alone* does not guarantee success.

----

[108] Schneider, Wolfgang. "Developmental trends in the metamemory-memory behavior relationship: An integrative review." *Metacognition, cognition, and human performance* 1 (1985): 57-109.

[109] Graham, Steve, and Karen R. Harris. "The role of self-regulation and transcription skills in writing and writing development." Educational psychologist 35.1 (2000): 3-12.

45. Strategies for Self-Regulation

Zimmerman's research, which was able to predict academic success with a 93% accuracy[110], lists 11 key learning skills which productive students consistently utilise.

These are explored more fully below, with references made to other sections of this book if they are covered elsewhere.

Note that true success of these relies upon the following stages being secure:
- Awareness of strategy
- Implementation
- Ability to select strategy appropriately across a range of contexts

As has been explored previously, one can assume that students should know to use certain strategies if they have been introduced to them, but the best indication of appropriate self-regulation is to select the right strategies unprompted, and use it across a variety of contexts. This is something which can be encouraged, hinted at and signposted, but the only way for this to be achieved is to have buy-in from the students themselves.

---

[110] Zimmerman, Barry J, and Manuel Martinez Pons. "Development of a structured interview for assessing student use of self-regulated learning strategies." *American educational research journal* 23.4 (1986): 614-628.

These skills and strategies are: self-evaluation, organisation, goal setting and planning, information seeking, record keeping, self-monitoring, environmental structuring, giving self-consequences, rehearsing and memorising, seeking social assistance and reviewing of text and notes.

Students who were able to rate their consistency in using them in their study were differentiated by their rate of academic success. This was unprompted recall of their studying attributes; self-regulation by its very nature can be driven by teachers but is fuelled by the students themselves. Giving these strategies alone is not enough; they should be accessed independently, and their beneficial values identified and recognised as suiting each particular task by the students.

It should also be noted that self-regulation forms just one part of academic success. Many of the strategies for learning in this book are codependent on each other for their long-term impact.

If one were to create a curriculum around self-regulation, it would be one which builds within the learning setting once introduced. In this way, students can adopt and adapt the different strategies to suit a wide variety of contexts; indeed, it is this skill of transferability between contexts which recognises the multitude of benefits they each bring.

46. Self-evaluation

Self-evaluation could be described as assessing performance against a personal goal, and self-reactions against those judgements.

Indeed, this is a definite move from teachers leading learning to students learning to be their own teacher. This could be seen as in a diametrically-opposed position from Direct Instruction, where the 'sage on stage' model has an enormous Effect Size, but in fact the two can co-exist together, just not at the same time (like two genres of music being favourable, just not together).

Much of the research regarding self-regulation indicates that is the student's' active participation in their own metacognition, motivation and behaviour; attributes which are identified by multiple studies as features of high-attaining students, which are not visible in low-attaining students. By active I mean that the students aren't just completing tasks because they want to, but rather because they have been 'sold' the inherent benefits of using these methods to improve and refine their learning in the future too.

The study of self-evaluation has grown from both studying those who use it actively, and from teaching the technique to those students struggling via an intervention, of which it is largely successful. These skills can be taught, learnt and put into practice effectively, alleviating low performance. This in turn goes some way to explaining the high Effect Size.

Self-evaluation consists of three goals, largely defined as:

- The overarching goal, broken into recognisable and adjustable stages
- Constant monitoring of performance against these mini-goals
- Making adjustments according to self-performance

Although summarised in three small phrases, this is incredibly hard to maintain. As a runner, I have become more and more aware of the way my mind will convince me to reduce my run if I am tired, bored or struggling, particularly on there-and-back runs. To that end, I now try and run loops or point-to-point, pre-selecting my route according to the distance I need to cover, so that I'm unable to withdraw at any point. This takes mental effort.

47. Goal setting

We can all set goals or accept goals from others. The language used in the UK climate in education is however rather flaccid in its own optimism - we tend to hear of learning intentions rather than learning goals.

Certainly to me, a learning goal is tangible, concrete and within reach (albeit perhaps just out of reach at the same time). An intention has much more to influence it. I may intend not to buy anything other than what is on my shopping list when I go to the supermarket; whether I achieve that or not is another matter.

There will be some teachers who worry that if we set high attaining goals for the students which they continually don't achieve, they can become despondent or disenfranchised. The glib yet honest response to this is to adjust the intentions according to your students. But this challenges our abilities to teach ambitious curriculum materials to all our students.

According to Mabe and West,[111] goals can be broken down into two very specific types:

- learning goals - also known as mastery or task goals
- achievement goals - ego or ability goals

---

[111] Mabe, Paul A, and Stephen G West. "Validity of self-evaluation of ability: A review and meta-analysis." *Journal of applied Psychology* 67.3 (1982): 280.

There are a multitude of studies identifying that students focussing on learning goals use deeper cognitive and metacognitive strategies, have more adaptive motivational beliefs, show greater levels of effort and persistence and are more willing to seek help. The table below characterises these two goals against each other.

As you will identify, one set of traits is demonstrably more attractive for our students than the other.

While these are very broad and generalist definitions of the traits exhibited, we should be able to recognise some of our key students in one or other camp. This is well within the realm of mindsets, and Carol Dweck[112] features in a number of meta analyses regarding self-goals[113].

Learning Goal Traits	Achievement Goal Traits
Able to elaborate their work Well organised Plans goals along route Observes own performance Believes they can achieve Enjoyment of tasks and learning Positive reactions to tasks High effort and persistence Seeks academic help	Can be restrictive Is generally organised Focussed on end goal Measures performance against others Belief defined by success Completes tasks for purpose Ticks tasks as they are completed Effort matched to need Outside help seen as weakness

[112] Carol Dweck rise to Educational fame largely began with her book, listed below, but spent many years researching the areas her book explored. She has since had to defend the Mindset approach, noting that some schools and teachers have taken what was intended out of context.

[113] Dweck, Carol. Mindset: The new psychology of success. Random House, 2006.

Further research into achievement goals found that the effects of these could be altered according to which objective predominates when approaching a task; demonstrating one's own competence, or avoiding negative judgements about self-worth[114].

If we consider some of the more able students that we teach, we are probably able to place them broadly in one of these two camps; or even ourselves. Although I would consider myself quite learning-oriented, I still recognise that some of my drive comes from the ego goal - and am aware that some online social habits help me to reward that goal, for example by sharing a run with others on Twitter or Facebook. Yet it's been found that students who operate with a primarily ego-oriented goal can demonstrate behavioural patterns which contribute to harmful learning and motivation. With your eye on the prize, you can quickly give up if you feel it is simply unobtainable; motivation crashes[115].

The cross-over between different areas of metacognition and self-regulation are never more apparent than here. The qualities which offer a more robust and substantial learner can be demonstrated, explored and celebrated, with recognition for using them (which Marzano encourages, on page 157). There is of course the disparity between this and the pressure which schools feel

[114] Harackiewicz, Judith M et al. "Predicting success in college: A longitudinal study of achievement goals and ability measures as predictors of interest and performance from freshman year through graduation." *Journal of Educational Psychology* 94.3 (2002): 562.

[115] Pintrich, Paul R. "Multiple goals, multiple pathways: The role of goal orientation in learning and achievement." *Journal of educational psychology* 92.3 (2000): 544.

increasingly under to deliver results. Place these goal traits against your own school values; are they all encouraged and demonstrated in your philosophies, culture and action plans?

Whilst it can be said that one set of these traits is preferable over another's, that is not to suggest that having a combination of these values isn't good. Indeed, learners who don't have any opinion on their eventual academic achievements are likely long term to find their drive eroding. It has been found that a focus on social goals, in coordination with academic goals is one of the most successful ways to increase learning and academic performance[116]. It is a mental adjustment from an AND statement to a BECAUSE statement - 'because I enjoy and plan my learning, I achieve well academically.'

---

[116] *Harackiewicz, Judith M., et al. "Revision of achievement goal theory: Necessary and illuminating." (2002): 638.*

48. Call LASSI for help

How then do we help our students to identify and measure these traits? The Learning and Study Strategies Inventory is one such tool which goes some way to helping with this difficult challenge.

Built as a self-reporting questionnaire, it compromises a range of items that students have to declare as suing or ignoring in their study strategies. The items are grouped into one of ten categories; attitude, motivation, time organisation, anxiety, concentration, information processing, selection of main ideas, use of techniques and support materials, self-assessment and testing strategies. Although the LASSI was devised by Weinstein et al. (1987), it correlates fairly comfortably with Zimmerman's research in the strategies students could themselves identify as successful for them, as the table overleaf demonstrates.

Now available as a self-marking questionnaire, the LASSI not only identifies the strengths of the students, but also provides feedback in what they need to do in order to become better strategic learners. It helps them identify which self-regulation techniques will most benefit their learning journey in a way that a teacher might have to more laboriously unpick and clarify weaker traits, and as Zimmerman found, students are statistically better at identifying weaknesses in their learning strategies than their teachers often are.

So how does identifying these traits help students to become effective learners, and what influence do they have individually

Zimmerman	LASSI
<ul><li>self-evaluation</li><li>organisation</li><li>goal setting</li><li>planning</li><li>information seeking</li><li>record keeping</li><li>self-monitoring</li><li>environmental structuring</li><li>giving self-consequences</li><li>rehearsing</li><li>memorising</li><li>seeking social assistance</li><li>reviewing of text and notes</li></ul>	<ul><li>attitude</li><li>motivation</li><li>time organisation</li><li>anxiety</li><li>concentration</li><li>information processing</li><li>selection of main ideas</li><li>use of techniques and support materials</li><li>self-assessment</li><li>testing strategies</li></ul>

and collectively? A study by Francisco Cano explored exactly that[117], grouping the ten LASSI scales and putting them in three distinct groups, carefully correlating them against achievement. What this uncovered was which of these broad traits had most influence over achievement - what trait worked best.

Although some traits were seen to fit more than one strategy, for simplicity I have shown only the main thread. The results can be found below. As can be hopefully gleaned from this, the three most influential studying strategies, particularly within the realm of self-regulation, are motivation, testing strategies and self-testing (when viewed as the most successful) from each overarching theme.

---

[117] Cano, Francisco. "An in-depth analysis of the Learning and Study Strategies Inventory (LASSI)." *Educational and Psychological Measurement* 66.6 (2006): 1023-1038.

What can we take and learn from this as teachers? While all of these areas are worthy of exploration in the classroom, identifying what motivates our students, how they approach their tests and

Strategy	Trait
Affective Strategies	Time Management (0.82) Motivation (0.86) Concentration (0.50) Attitude (0.39)
Goal Strategies	Negative Anxiety (0.63) Test Strategies (0.71) Selecting main ideas (0.70)
Comprehension monitoring Strategies	Information processing (0.54) Self-testing (0.68) Study Aids (0.63)

they monitor their own progress through self-testing are three key goals in the journey to self-regulation.

Note: The figure in brackets refers to 'Standard maximum likelihood estimations of correlation'

In exploring self-regulation with regard to these traits, it is worth considering the time given to nurturing and emphasising these traits in your teaching. We can expect, especially in the latter years of Education, students to be fully conversant in them merely through exposure, yet this preconception can often be wrong - simply seeing something or being asked to do something enough times does not correlate with understanding it or using it as a wise learning strategy.

Indeed, much of my frustration when I first used story maps (see page 96) with my class was directed at their inability to make notes rather than start writing the story out in full, as they were want to do. I had expected them at this age to simply know what I meant by making notes; an assumption which led to a lowering of my expectations of them upon delivery, and a failed objective. Had I first identified that they were poor at making notes, shown them some techniques, and then asked them to make notes within a story framework concept I would have had a more successful outcome (albeit with a longer initial timeframe).

As with almost all of the strategies in this book, initial investment creates gains in the long term; much of the effort with these tasks is front-loaded.

49. Learning Habits Questionnaire

While the LASSI questionnaire is commercially available, there is no reason at all why you cannot create your own version of the questionnaire for your own cohort, using the different categories suggested.

I did exactly this at my old School, and the questions I used can be found overleaf. Note that these were written specifically for my own students, so you may want to change the wording, order or language, or simply use this is as a good starting point for your own questionnaire.

To make life easier for myself, I used the frankly brilliant Google Forms feature of Google Drive (currently found in Google Sheets) to create my questionnaire[118]. This allows you to make any type of questionnaire with ease.

In addition, it collates the results for you to either analyse automatically, or you can select individuals, cohorts or classes to analyse and then plan appropriate interventions.

---

[118] Any readers who would like to see this online version can request it using mr.lockyer@gmail.com

I carried the test out myself, and it highlighted my issues both with concentration and anxiety. While these were not a surprise to me, it is likely that some of your students will be surprised by what results the questionnaire brings up.

For ease of data collection, I used the Likert Scale, from 1 (Unlike me) to 5 (Completely me). Although this can encourage vagueness with a string of 3s (neutral), I found that the results I got from the students were more accurate with more choices given. Statisticians will probably disagree.

Name   Date:

Class: Year:

Gender: Date of Birth:

Part 1: Time Management

I don't often feel the pressure of time

I am able to plan my work

I complete homework with time to spare

Teachers give me enough time to finish tasks

I rarely run out of time

Use the class clock to help me ensure I stay on task

Part 2: Concentration

I find concentrating easy

I'm not easily distracted

I find the classroom an easy place to concentrate

I can maintain my focus throughout a task

I can concentrate for extended periods of time

Part 3: Attitude

I am determined to do well at school

I believe my teachers want me to achieve

I don't allow other children to distract me from learning

I am willing to ask for help if I need it

Part 4: Negative Anxiety

I don't get nervous when I'm under pressure

I don't let worry stop me from working

I don't find easier tasks to do when stuck

I can get stressed but know how to calm myself

I recognise when I might feel myself becoming anxious

Part 5: Test Strategies

I feel prepared when I am about to complete a test

I enjoy taking tests

I am able to mark questions I am unsure of, and return to them later

I am aware how to organise my time during a test

I can check through my work carefully to identify errors

I like to see what I have done well and what I can improve on after tests

Part 6: Selecting main ideas

I like to consider the main ideas of a topic

I can identify the main features

I read headings and Contents Pages carefully

I like to read around a subject or find out more

Part 7: Selecting Main Ideas

I can identify the main themes of a topic

I can argue for or against a theme

Given a theme, I can produce some subtopics

I am able to explain the main ideas in a topic

Part 8: Information Processing

I can select good sources of information to help me

I am able to work out reliable sources of information

I can identify where information comes from

I can explain why something might be a poor information source

I can make notes from a lot of text

Part 9: Self-testing

I am able to set myself challenges

I can write questions to help test my knowledge

I can explain my thinking to my teacher and other students

I set myself mini tests to help my learning

I am able to complete challenges I set myself

If I get something wrong, I go over it until I understand fully

Part 10: Study Aids

I can study effectively

I use study aids such as diagrams to help me learn

I can explain my thinking using illustrations and notes

I have effective revision strategies

I can read over my book and notes to help me study

Please write down the things you do to make sure you are learning to your best:

50. Feeding Learning Goals

The traits of a student who operates using learning goals as their primary motivation enable that student to succeed, or fail, with comfort. So how does a teacher encourage these traits in their students?

Below are some strategies to enhance learning goals for students. This is not an exhaustive list, and a quick search online will offer many more innovative ways in which staff in schools help students to identify the most successful ways to adopt these goals for themselves. Much of the leap for the student is trust in the teacher, and the method itself, so real life examples and active, daily demonstrations work incredibly effectively. By their very nature, many examples of learning goals in action are stories, which are always much easier to recall than data points or pithy slogans on motivational posters - though there is always a place for these too.

Able to elaborate their work

Stretching their work beyond 'what was asked' is a perennial challenge for teachers. Having the children work on improving their own tasks, looking at other people's tasks and giving advice and guidance on improvement is a fantastic way of helping the children to elaborate their work and make them think about refinement techniques. A key skill here is questioning; asking children deeper questions which encourage open answers forces the child to think carefully and judiciously about their choices, justifying decisions and making incremental improvements.

Well organised

It is easy to appreciate that a well-organised student is more able to learn, and find teaching more accessible to them. However, organisation skills need to be taught to the children and demonstrated through highlighting and good practice in order for the children to understand the benefits of organisation. Some children find organisation incredibly hard, so streamlining everything they have to do makes their work improvement rate increase and removes unnecessary distractions. Make all the equipment that children need to complete a task easily accessible, labelled if necessary. Highlight this to the class at the beginning of any task, so they know not only what is available to them and where it is, but also as a gentle reminder they may need these tools.

Plans goals along route

Breaking down one large goal into smaller, more manageable goals, is an incredibly effective way of measuring progress along a given route. A 1000 word essay seems far more daunting than 10 100 word written tasks for example. even in the primary setting, showing an overall goal and encouraging the children to create smaller key goals along the route will help them to measure their success and achievement at each stage towards the overall goal.

Observes own performance

We are acutely able to seemingly make judgements on other people's performances, often at the cost of our own performance. Indeed, one of my son's end-of-year reports stated that he *"can sometimes concentrate more on everyone else's progress, at a cost of his own,"* a phrase which I'm sure would have appeared on my own school reports at the same age.

Too often, students operate using only two broad questions underlining their performance:

- What am I doing now?
- What do I have to do next?

These are fairly closed questions, and are rather simple to ask oneself. What they give no indication of is a measure of how they can improve either of the 'what' statements. They are functional and offer no measure of performance technique.

By encouraging students to adjust these regular self questions, we can encourage them to become better observers at their own performance. This of course depends on them changing their course, should they need to, rather than ploughing on in a direction which completes the task set without making any change, however small or incremental. Consider these two questions instead:

- How am I getting on now?
- How can I change what I am doing to ensure I am achieving the most?

With achievement in this last question being both academic achievement (completing the task) as well as learning achievement (is there anything that can be done to make my learning more beneficial for the future), these questions go some way to developing a mentality that performance should be regularly looked at, analysed and changed if necessary.

The quickest way to do this is to prompt the students to consider these two questions as they work through a task. Have the two questions written on the board or on a poster, and stop the class every five minutes to ask them what they think are the answers, and what they are going to do about each of them. This tiny change can have very broad implications for deeper learning and understanding within a task, and carrying this out in all lessons will help to lasso the idea of measuring self-performance in the student's minds.

Belief that they can achieve

Another popular educational meme is one about failure; *"if you knew you wouldn't fail, what things would you do?"* The answer of course is (or should be) nothing. There is no point in me attempting to be the world's fastest man, as I just don't have the drive, ambition, ability, determination, body shape or required narcissism to achieve this. I will cope.

How many of our students feel that many of the challenges they are set are beyond them, and don't attempt to achieve because they already know that despite everything they do, they are heading helplessly toward failure? To answer this, we need to question the way in which the student both is given their self-belief, and also in the way that achievement is positioned within our classroom culture.

One simple device I have used in the past is the "Portfolio of Excellence." This was a large ring-bound folder of past student work. It was known by the students to exist, and they were regularly shown completed tasks be former students. The impact it had was incredible in helping the students believe that they could achieve. Not only could they see examples of work which former students had done, it was also shown what good completed work looked like; the task was achievable.

After trialling this in my own classroom, I rolled this out across the school for all subjects. This had the added benefits of not only helping teachers to align what they accepted as good work ("is this work good enough to go in the Portfolio of Excellence?") which in turn fed down to the students as a form of carrot; would their work be good enough to go into the Portfolio.

In addition, these folders produced an excellent set of examples of good practice for Inspectors to look at when they inevitably visited my school. They could see both our expectations of the students and these expectations delivered in work. This was our work ethos exemplified in practice, and enabled us to secure the highest rating against their criteria.

Enjoyment of tasks and learning

This seems to be so obvious as to not warrant even mentioning, and yet how do we know, or even measure, whether a student is enjoying learning or not? To my mind, enjoyment equates to actual desire to learn, rather than have the learning somehow foisted upon them. As Dave Burgess puts it in his 2012 book, *'Teach Like a Pirate'*[119], "If students had the choice of attending your lessons, how many would be empty?"

This is not, I should emphasise, to provide teaching which is somehow entertaining or of such a performance that the teacher takes precedence over learning. Rather, providing tasks and learning which hooks in the students' interest and curiosity in the given subject all help to contribute to enjoyment; we can go back to considering learning to be like the 'charged' self-propelling toy car rather than the one which we are constantly having to nudge along.

---

[119] Burgess, Dave. Teach Like a Pirate: Increase Student Engagement, Boost Your Creativity and Transform Your Life as an Educator. Dave Burgess Consulting, 2012.

Enjoyment is hard to measure and yet easy to identify; it is that moment where students have their own drive to continue, ask questions and want to progress at a rate which matches or exceeds the teacher's own expectations. Given two tasks to do at home, I am almost always more likely to select the one which I derive more pleasure from, but these are all context driven to a certain extent (note how tidy my house is during report-writing time for example).

Rather than considering if the work or learning is 'fun,' ask instead if the work arouses enough interest or curiosity to encourage an independent drive from the students to want to know more or contribute more.

Positive reactions to tasks

There should be a reaction to all tasks whether positive or negative. It is the adjustment of focus for this which enables us as teachers to identify whether this reaction is positive or not. Simply completing a task because it has been set seems to be a more common pattern in school. That is not to criticise the teacher for setting tasks, but encouraging and enabling a positive reaction to tasks in the classroom setting so that it goes some way to matching the enthusiasm and positivity which students exhibit outside the classroom (toward their hobbies for example) offers short term gains and much larger long-term benefits.

One measure of adeptness the teacher can have is to 'read' the reaction of a task from the students. If they are raring to go, and forsake lesson niceties in order to begin the task, we can be aware that this particular task has 'got them.' Likewise, if a task can be aligned with one of their preferred working styles, and it is not detrimental to their learning opportunities, a teacher would be wise to marry these two together.

One colleague, knowing the set text she was asked by the exam board to teach was tricky to access, instead covered the initial grounds using character study, different situations involving dilemmas and some initial historical grounding before introducing the set text. In this way, she was able to allow the students make the connection between their interests (which had been fed) to the text, rather than jumping straight into a challenging text to begin with. As a result, she gained much greater buy-in from her students.

High effort and persistence

These are really two leaves of the same plant, and in my experience can both be much misunderstood by the students in class. What actually is high effort? When asking students what they thought this meant, the few I spoke to came back with "working harder." This is a pat phrase however; almost devoid of meaning when it is considered. To give an example, imagine a student is completing a page of long division sums. Using this concept of "work harder," what do we actually expect the students to do?

- complete more sums
- work faster
- get less distracted
- finish faster than others

Of these four reasons, perhaps only the one about distraction has any validity. Working faster can often lead to mistakes in some tasks. So what is high effort?

The dictionary definition of "effort" is that of a 'determined attempt,' which is contrary to many of the work harder strategies listed above. Effort in this sense isn't skipping the hard question, or hoping the answer you have placed is right without checking it - it is taking a pause and taking stock and telling yourself (as a student) if you have approached that particular challenge as one to successfully beat, or one which may get a cross, but which doesn't really matter.

This is of course incredibly hard to do. Given the example above, but especially when all the class are completing the same broad task, it seems to be only natural when set that the aim of the task is to 'complete the sheet' rather than 'refine your long division method.' again, what does this actually mean for a student? To my mind, this could be expanded as:

- secure your understanding of long division across a range of examples
- Recognise errors through self-checking
- Place this method against a range of contexts (ie in word problems, real life problems and in solving long divisions in other subjects).

Instead, what can often happen is we mark the work, highlighting the errors and asking the student to repeat them. This is when the cost of marking after a lesson, rather than during a lesson has a great cost. It's rather like driving from Halfords after an MOT, then at home being told you need new bulbs. The learning MOT needs to be carried out within the lesson.

One successful strategy I have used to great effect in this type of task is to scan the work covered by the student and tell them that they have made three errors - but not tell them where they are. Cynics of my analogies might at this juncture point out that this is akin to failing your MOT but not being told what your car has failed on - which is a fair charge if I'm honest.

What I have found however is that it makes the student go over their work again in a slightly frustrated but different mentality, that of a fact-checker rather than a task-completer. It is very difficult for students to utilise these two strategies next to each other, which is broadly speaking what more effort requires, yet encouraging this practice is really beneficial for the students.

Having the students write 'checked' and signing their names against every column or row might work as a way of both encouraging them to focus on checking, whilst making them accountable for the checking, rather than the teacher.

Persistence is rather different - this is a mark of doggedness to complete, rather than giving up. As a semi-professional procrastinator, who can argue that any failure in productivity is the fault of either hunger pangs or Netflix, I know only too well that our resistance to proceed diminishes when we find something hard. So where does grit come from; that desire to continue despite adversity?

To my mind, it firstly needs the acknowledgement that work should be intrinsically hard. There is almost no charm in work being easy to complete.

Struan Robertson, in his book 'Lower your life handicap'[120] wrote that the ability to get a hole-in-one at every golf course would remove the central pleasure of golf itself. The key aspect here is removing the sense of helplessness that situations making someone feel they can't proceed, and allowing them to recognise what they need to do next - and just getting on with it!

---

[120] "Lower your life handicap" by Struan Robertson, 2015, Be-A-Ten

This message isn't well-received by students or adults however - as I can personally identify. Persistence, coupled with self-goals such as self-motivation and self-evaluation, can help enormously. This can be done by asking oneself a few questions, namely:

- What am I stuck on?
- What is preventing me from giving my all?
- What can I change to make me continue?

By answering these questions honestly, both you and the student can help to redefine persistence and ensure that you both are working on a task or goal which can be broken down into much more manageable chunks.

Seeks academic help

There seems to be a drive toward independent learning which puts the teacher at the end of the asking circuit - "see three before me" and so on. The overarching aim of this is to encourage students to think beyond simply putting their hands up and asking questions that perhaps they or a peer know the answer to. The danger of this well-intentioned guidance as this it places the teacher at the far end of support. While this is worthy, it does force a certain isolation for the teacher as some knowledge deity who should not be disturbed at all costs.

This is a pattern which appears to grow in stature as students get older. Rather than it being reversed, teachers should be viewed as accessible, especially for certain tasks and activities. What should a teacher be viewed as, which is a source for guidance beyond "which question is next?" and rather tackles worries the student may have, or helps to unlock the next level of learning. Teachers therefore need to ensure that students do see them as a source of academic assistance; that they are approachable and accessible for the learning.

51. Sight Unseen: Thinking Aloud

As a form of hearing and understanding the cognitive processes underlying any process, the technique of think-aloud is almost unprecedented in its impact.

Indeed, in his book about this[121], Maarten Someren highlights this explicitly, drawing in the research carried out which demonstrated the four basic protocols in problem solving (analysing the current problem, proposing a solution, implementing a solution and evaluating the solution) importantly noting that just one of these is visible when judging end work alone.

The aspect of keeping a sketchbook of ideas and these processes appears to be the sole domain of Art students, and actually contribute to the overall grade a student can gain in GCSE or A Level in this subject; their grade is in part due to them setting out their thinking process itself. With only 25% of some marks being awarded for the final piece itself, it could be fair to rebrand Art as Art Thinking courses.

 While other subjects may demand some examples of the thinking process behind answers, the Art sketchbook is perhaps most clear it its aims of mapping out the journey to an end piece of work, from initial ideas (and rejection of some ideas) to evaluating the finished piece. Why then is this the preserve of Art alone? Would

---

[121] Van Someren, Maarten W., Yvonne F. Barnard, and Jacobijn AC Sandberg. The think aloud method: A practical guide to modelling cognitive processes. Vol. 2. London: Academic Press, 1994.

we not gain a huge amount as teachers to see or hear the thinking behind answers in English, Maths or Geography for example? Wouldn't it be easier to identify errored thinking in the students, or see exactly where they lost sight of their initial target? Instead we request incrementally-improved results, without often discovering the thinking behind these results.

If we take problem-solving as the overarching learning aim, we can hopefully agree that two students can take any number of routes in finding a common and correct answer. What then does the teacher gain understanding the processes behind solving the problem for each of the students with a solitary answer? Nothing.

Taken at face value, this is more than simply a teacher to explain their thinking processes out loud. In order to gain real value, the teacher needs to analyse their responses, and consider best whether to:

- intervene and re-align thinking of the student
- provide prompts to give the student a better direction
- listen to the process, identifying strategies which need further input or support

This is teaching as a surgical tool, not as a judging tool. Leah Sharp, a Year 6 teacher in Worthing, uses video clips of Paul Hollywood and Mary Berry to help model effective feedback for her students, yet she also recognises that the closer this feedback is to the deed, the more beneficial it is at that moment in time. Knowing that you haven't been careful enough in weighing your ingredients is useful for the future, but knowing this before you put your cake in the oven is far more useful. A key aspect then of thinking-aloud is the preserve of the teaching giving this direct feedback, rather than delayed feedback, which equates to judgement.

In his book, Someren uses the term 'knowledge engineer' which I immediately became besotted with, describing as it does someone who acquires information and then does something with it. It is far from the idea of 'knowledge conveyor' which we may perhaps be more guilty of building, with students being fed information to then spout out in another form. This is a broad judgement of course, and the optimistic character in me suspects that many teachers' intentions are to build engineers and not conveyors. Do our lessons, school culture and actions reflect this belief?

52. How to use think-aloud in the classroom

This technique is one which highlights the benefits which modelling can produce when carried out by a teacher. It is a technique I used an awful lot in maths, when explaining a particular strategy, but not so much in other subjects, when I 'just knew' the end point and told the children how to get there.

By modelling think-aloud as teachers, we are sharing with our students the right things to say in terms of the problem-solving protocols above. Note that we are not explaining the procedure of something, which is often a series of 'then you' statements, but rather, we are distilling down our actual thinking, making suggestions and ideas, and being honest in regression or rejection of ideas.

If you ask students to carry out some think-aloud without careful modelling beforehand, you end up with the basic 'then-you' procedure mentioned above. What is simply happening is an event commentary or process overview, which is useful but doesn't bring the benefits we would hope to bring with think-aloud.

Let us consider for a moment an insulation challenge in a Science lesson, where students have to assemble a container to maintain the temperature of a container holding boiling water for as long as possible. When constructed by the teacher, with them thinking aloud, here is a possible monologue they might hear.

"So I have a range of materials that I can use to insulate my container. I know that some of these are better than others at insulating, as they are used for other insulating purposes. This fluff looks like the fluff in my winter coat, which I know keeps me warm, so I think this has high insulating property. I think my best bet here is to remove the items I think which don't insulate well, and then order than ones I do."

Here, the teacher is giving references to real-life examples of insulation, they are talking about what they might do first, and beginning to identify that some of the materials they might have are no good.

When the students attempt this challenge themselves, they are now more able to think-aloud the way they would solve the problem (which in this case can have many solutions). They are more comfortable rejecting materials (as the teacher has done), and know that by thinking aloud, they are sharing with their peers the processes and decisions they are coming to in advance, rather than having to defend them afterwards.

Think-aloud exemplifies the power that using an active approach to thinking can have. It utilises the traits of an effective learner, it encourages the rejection of initial but invalid ideas (to no detriment to the learner) and helps the teacher see which processes are refined, and which need support.

It may be helpful to define rules for think-aloud in your classroom, especially when this is a new concept. Any idea which encourages exploration as part of its strategy is also going to make the occasional mistake, so an environment where students experience comfort in 'feeling around' a problem or topic needs to have the reassurance that good thinking does take the odd wrong turn.

The think-aloud method has much more variance and nuance than is outlined here, and I would recommend you read *"The Think-Aloud Method"* book. It covers the technique with reference to both learning, and how to build computer-responsive systems using think-aloud as a research method. We can for example input ailments into a computer, but interviewing and recording real doctors' analysis of ailments can help to forge new, and more accurate, paths to diagnosis using a computer system. A free .PDF of the book is available online[122].

---

[122] Van Someren, Maarten W, Yvonne F Barnard, and Jacobijn AC Sandberg. *The think aloud method: A practical guide to modelling cognitive processes*. London: Academic Press, 1994.

53. Self-Planning

What opportunities do we give students to genuinely plan their own work? How often do we as teachers subconsciously give the students a model of planning which largely consists of "complete this task" or even "finish this task" in our lessons?

To help students, we need to encourage them to develop planning strategies which enable them to develop a form of self-assessment. This is done by breaking down tasks further than simply 'complete,' into stages which feel both within reach and accomplishable.

There is of course a fine line between independent working and scaffolding, where the teacher isn't handholding but rather shining the learning torch both ways - looking back at previous work and highlighting the next stages.

We as teachers need to build into our students the willingness to stop, take stock of the stages achieved so far, and evaluate what they need to do next in order to make the most of the learning opportunities ahead of them. Here is a sample procedure to help planning:

- What have I done?
- What (specific elements) did I find hard?
- How did I resolve this?
- How can this help me to make better progress in the next?

- What can I do to plan this into my future learning?

These questions may need help and guidance at first; model them for your students in a way that they feel comfortable in answering them honestly, and explain how they might better plan their learning. If this period of self-evaluation highlights for example that their greatest number of errors thus far is a lack of capital letters in their work, ensure they add checking of these in planning future work.

When introducing this to students, it is good to utilise a method which they can easily replicate in other subjects and contexts. Pause, aPpraise and Plan is a simple mnemonic which emphasises the key stages of good planning:

Pause - don't continue for the moment but assess and take stock of work produced thus far.

aPpraise - evaluate the work produced and view against either given criteria, or self-goals (goals set by the students themselves). Is the work acceptable? What needs to change, or be expanded? Does the future work need to go in a different direction?

Plan - rather than leaping straight back into the task, plan out (using notes and timings if necessary) what steps need to be taken in order to complete the next stage of the task.

It is often the case that students find it hard to plan - again, this is a skill which needs to be taught rather than assumed. Talking through actually how to plan the next stages with students can benefit their understanding and expectations of the planning stage.

54. Computer-assisted instruction

This represents a classic metacognition chicken-and-egg dilemma: does computer-assisted instruction encourage greater thinking skills, or do stronger thinking skills aid computer-assisted instruction?

It's an interesting argument, since if computer-assisted instruction, or CAI as it is more easily referred to, was to improve greater thinking skills, this would make the implementation of metacognition into schools easier, since it is taken as read that there is firstly the infrastructure in place to facilitate this, and the computational thinking behind metacognitive processes would have been already distilled into the program, rather than having to train up the teachers.

What has been found is that testing of students who enrolled in a computer programming course lasting just 12 weeks found that these students have performed significantly higher when measured against the control group (who simply studied CAI) in terms of reflectivity and divergent thinking, scoring higher on measures of metacognitive ability and the ability to describe directions. This study found however that there were no differences on cognitive development[123].

So we know that specific programs, especially those which involve programming, can assist in encouraging metacognitive ability - the ability to think about thinking. So what actually works in the classroom, and can computers be the metacognition panacea that Schools perhaps want but don't realise they want?

What is challenging about this question is the speed of change and evolution in this area. While many techniques described in this book have been around for many decades (in some cases, thousands of years), and so have been researched and explored by research institutes, computing and programming has a history of only a few decades, and is at such a pace that research has admittedly struggled to keep up.

One recent meta-analysis[124] looking at both cognitive impact and computing found only seven valid studies, with almost all dating to the 1980s and 1990s - some years before most of our students were even born, perhaps even some of their parents.

This puts some doubt in their findings for today's generation of learners who, certainly in the Western World, have ready access to information and technology in a format that we could perhaps not have even conceived ten years ago. We may not have the

---

[123] Clements, Douglas H, and Dominic F Gullo. "Effects of computer programming on young children's cognition." *Journal of Educational Psychology* 76.6 (1984): 1051.

[124] Scruggs, Thomas E et al. "Do special education interventions improve learning of secondary content? A meta-analysis." *Remedial and Special Education* 31.6 (2010): 437-449.

hoverboards which *Back to The Future* promised us in 2015, but our children can visit their Australian relatives virtually on FaceTime, buy and read books online and modify games which are bought without any physical packaging.

The things we can learn about the benefits of metacognition from using CAI using these older research papers is still interesting, and do paint a picture of which direction this area may be heading, if not an accurate summary of what the situation is now.

What research has shown[125] is that the Effect Size changes according to the age who is experiencing CAI. Unlike what you might expect, the Effect Size decreases as the student ages, as seen in the table below.

Setting	Effect Size
Special School	0.56
Primary School	0.46
Secondary School	0.32
College/University	0.26

This is very interesting, and contrary to what one might consider to be the case - surely exposure to computers and technology grows as the student ages, leading to a greater effect? It is perhaps this exposure which causes the decrease however - there is a novelty in using technology which possibly becomes less novel as the ubiquity increases; the more you use it, the less impact it has. What is apparent from these figures however is that Special Schools, who cater for all ages, indicated an Effect Size

---

[125] Niemiec, Richard P, Christian Sikorski, and Herbert J Walberg. "Learner-control effects: A review of reviews and a meta-analysis." *Journal of Educational Computing Research* (1996).

greater than all others. Is there something about learning through technology rather than a human which allows a greater focus or appeal for the students?

The impact on time also has an effect when using technology compared to conventional teaching, with a rough estimate that learning something through technology takes around 70% of the time than through teaching. Put simply, a ten hour course can be covered in seven hours, with statistically better outcomes, if you remove the teacher.

This is the kind of research which tends to break my heart, before I get agitated and middle-class angry (read, quietly seething inside with no external signs of any annoyance). What is important to note is that the research which supports this statistic[126] looks at tests as an academic measure. They cover no nuance or influence the teacher brings to the classroom. We as teachers have no fear of being replaced by technology; at least, not until they find a way to add all the intangible value a human dimension to teaching brings to the classroom.

Teachers do still have an influence on the impact of computer interventions, with effect sizes greater for those who were taught by a different teacher to their normal teacher. While this is more common in Secondary and College education, it is an area which Primary Schools are increasingly willing to explore. The role of a subject-specific teacher is one in which I was for 11 years as a teacher and a role that I found rewarding on many levels.

---

[126] Kulik, Chen-Lin C, and James A Kulik. "Effectiveness of computer-based instruction: An updated analysis." *Computers in human behavior* 7.1 (1991): 75-94.

What influence does time have on learning in these situations? Certainly, it has been ascertained that mastery status is gained in a shorter time when students use technology[127], but also that a short intervention using computers (for example, on a Reading Recovery Program) has more impact than that of a longer course - the optimum length of time being four weeks. One would have thought that the effect size would have increased over time, when the research very clearly indicates otherwise. This is due in part to the Hawthorne Effect (page 30), that of the novelty itself of intervention, but also it is believed due to the focus that a shorter intervention brings. Anecdotally, we can ascribe to the belief that a short, sharp and focused intervention brings a high reward which isn't sustained over a longer period.

There are three broad types of computer application students have access to which make a difference to their cognitive functioning. They are:

- Computer-assisted Instruction (CAI) - drill-and-practice exercises
- Computer-mentored Instruction (CMI) - programs which evaluate test performance, guide students and keep a record of progress
- Computer-Enriched Instruction (CEI) - programs which serve as a problem-solving tool, generating data at the student's request, and executes their programs

Of these, the last is perhaps the most interesting in terms of metacognitive progress, and one specific area, that of the influence of learning to program, is one which has the most research and focus in the current curriculum drive.

[127] Guskey, Thomas R, and Therese D Pigott. "Research on group-based mastery learning programs: A meta-analysis." *The Journal of Educational Research* 81.4 (1988): 197-216.

55. Turtle Recall

The simplistic LOGO program, where students from an early age input instructions to move a turtle around the screen, hides a multitude of benefits for the user which are in addition to teaching them basic programming.

Freely available since the late 1960s, LOGO is a free download on all Operating Systems and devices, under a wide range of guises. There is a huge range in the Apple Appstore, the Android Marketplace and in the Chrome Webstore, and as with all new Apps, there very little physical programming using a keyboard with these - many of them have buttons to press or elements to drag. It is easier than ever to use LOGO.

At its heart, LOGO requires users to move a turtle around a blank space. He leaves a trail (why they didn't use a snail as the animal still puzzles me) behind him, although this can also be programmed to 'off,' follows direction changes using degree angles, and can repeat a given set of instructions. More complex versions of LOGO can have the turtle interact with other elements, react to parts of the screen and even take outside influences such as changes in sound, light or touch.

As with many things, the simplicity belies the power it can have, and much of the research in computing influences on metacognition centres around the use of LOGO. Its low-entry access and general ubiquity have helped this status.

One study[128] conducted with 6-8 year old children found that, when compared to using computer-assisted instruction or no computer use at all, those students on a LOGO programming course scored significantly higher when tested on their operational competence and creativity. In addition, they were statistically better at describing directions (which makes sense), and in several metacognitive skills. Significantly, there were no differences found in measures on their reading or mathematical achievement.

The most surprising result from this study was for me the increase in creativity. I believe that there is a perception that computing, and especially programming, tend not to be creative pursuits. Having worked alongside computer designers and programmers, I know this is not the case - programming is problem-solving personified to a certain degree. Yet when there are arguments for children using computers less as it makes them less creative, research such as this encourages me that this isn't the case. As with everything, moderation and support are two important parenting and teaching skills when it comes to children and computers.

Part of the connection between metacognition and LOGO is that it requires students to reflect on how they might complete a task, projecting how they themselves think[129]. By learning from their

[128] Battista, Michael T., and Douglas H. Clements. "The effects of Logo and CAI problem-solving environments on problem-solving abilities and mathematics achievement." Computers in Human Behavior 2.3 (1986): 183-193.

[129] Papert, Seymour. Mindstorms: Children, computers, and powerful ideas. Basic Books, Inc., 1980.

errors, students using LOGO are effectively debugging their thinking. Extending this idea, it is suggested by some that detecting errors forces shifts in attention to more important aspects[130].

As with many activities to encourage metacognition, dialogue between students, and between the teacher and the student, can be rich when using LOGO and other programming environments. These conversations can help to implement our own thinking or learn from others, and some research has shown that working on technology in pairs has more benefits than working with a device independently.

This is of course not to say that we can simply sit students in front of LOGO and magical metacognitive dust pours from the device. This program seems to work well within a specified age group, on specifically-focussed parts of metacognition (creativity and problem solving).

What is interesting about this first study is that you might have assumed that the problem-solving aspect would have been skewed toward geometric puzzles, the challenge was actually far more abstract.

"The thief who always wore disguises stole some money from bank. The detective saw a man dressed like a mailman run out of the bank with the money and drive away in a mail truck, but he couldn't catch him. Another day, money was stolen from another bank. The detective saw a tow truck drive away. He found three suspects dressed like: a garbage man, a gas station man, and a

---

[130] Dehn, Natalie, and Roger Schank. "Artificial and human intelligence." Handbook of human intelligence 1 (1982): 352-391.

fireman. The fireman had a wallet with some money in it. The garbage man looked mean. How could the detective prove who was the thief?"

I'm imagining you had to read that twice. This was the question given to eight-year olds, and the researchers recorded the answers given (they were asked to suggest questions the detective could ask the men).

This research was backed up by a similar study[131] carried out in Indonesia, where an older cohort were given an 8 week course in LOGO. The resulting gains when the students were tests was impressive; the students achieved significantly higher scores in tests covering problem-solving, creativity, thinking flexibility and originality.

This reflects something of LOGOs original aims, which was built around both programming and Piaget's theories of child development. LOGOs apparent 5 minute learning curve hides a multitude of powerful skills the students using it can refine by experimenting, creating shapes and solving problems. As the study's authors put it:

---

[131] Pardamean, Bens, Evelin Evelin, and Honni Honni. "The effect of logo programming language for creativity and problem solving." *Proceedings of the 10th WSEAS international conference on E-Activities* 1 Dec. 2011: 151-156.

"Planning the turtle's movements provides students with experience in how they think and learn. This higher-level thought process applied to a concrete object teaches them content, thinking styles, and behaviours needed for academic success."

This thinking comes through in a number of ways, and creates a useful casual tick list for programs which claim to encourage thinking skills.

Creativity - the creativity exhibited in these studies, and by LOGO users in general, comes from being forced to use a small but specific set of rules to control the turtle and thus create shapes. An analogue analogy would be the Etch-A-Sketch, where your drawing pen was even more restricted; you couldn't let it leave the screen. Given this versus free reign with a piece of paper and a pen, it is easy to see why there is more forward planning needed with LOGO over the latter, yet it isn't so easy to join the connection to creativity.

When measured in studies, this almost intangible quality was graded by looking at a picture created on LOGO (via building up several shapes to form a fuller picture) against one drawn free-hand. It is assumed in both cases that children knew about regular and irregular 2D shapes.

Problem solving - Whether guided or not, the LOGO environment is one where progress is based around solving problems, in a wide range of disciplines. To improve, you need to develop better direction skills, estimating skills, angle recognition, number scale, place value. Problem solving in this environment encourages exploration in geometry, spatial relations, properties of figures and visual reasoning.

LOGO lends itself well to research about computing and metacognition, but it doesn't exclude other programs and apps which can recreate (and even, further) the desirable outcomes which LOGO appears to produce. In my own home, Minecraft is acutely celebrated for its creativity, and I have seen first hand the manner in which it encourages problem-solving. Many educators around the world are also aware of its potency within learning opportunities, and the first noises of research including Minecraft are starting to emerge.

CONCLUSION

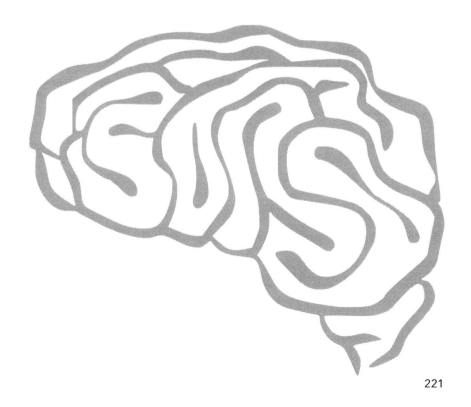

Conclusions

To structure this, I've returned to the original guiding principles (as I saw them) of Metacognition and Self-regulation programmes to be run by teachers or schools.

Teaching - If these are to have any impact in schools, these skills need to be explicitly taught. Teachers need to not simply pick up this book and run with the many practical ideas; rather they should devise an actual programme specific to their school (or employ someone to do this), carefully designing sessions for classes or small groups to benefit from. An ideal timetable would use one thirty minute period each week for all Junior classes. That is 120 sessions in a child's time at school - but the impact of this would be enormous, and the gains, though difficult to measure, would be immense.

Strategies - Although it is assumed that teachers will use some, if not many of these strategies already, it cannot be emphasised enough that using them in isolation has far less impact than taking a whole school approach - where every teacher and student knows how to use many different strategies *and* can employ them effectively for learning. This needn't be arduous and could well give teachers some new ways to tackle topics they normally find challenging or dry.

Gains - Many of the research papers evidenced in this book indicate gains over a longer period of time than many quick-fix solutions. Giving time to metacognition and self-regulation is a front-loaded investment of time, so will need the commitment of

Senior Leaders and Governors in order to be made a success. Creating a programme of study and committing to it over a period of years will deliver the best results for all students and teachers; the difficulty is that the gains may not be in evidence in Year 1.

Student Buy-in - This is essential for any metacognition strategy to work - students have to genuinely believe that they can improve and learn better, and approach different activities (such as group work) with possibly a different dynamic than one they are used to exhibiting. Almost all the strategies outlined require buy-in from the students, and any school who wants to seriously invest in metacognition programmes would to well to seek partnerships and support from parents too. The path to self-regulation is students becoming in charge of their own teaching and learning, which can be found in most school aims and objectives.

Teachers - While they juggle many different demands and expectations, teacher's lessons will benefit long-term from using metacognitive strategies. They will help to embed their learning and understanding, and will support their future learning too, given the right coaching. Often, teachers will already use some of these methods; adopting more doesn't feel too painful.

Goals - It cannot be underestimated how useful setting self-goals can be for students - this is a thread which runs through this book. Setting a simple, vocal self-goal for achievement and reviewing it is the first stage to making this a more natural, and automatic, practice.

Intervention - The link between learning difficulties and learning strategies is clear, and hopefully this book has persuaded some teachers to try a different approach with some learners for whom they show a flair, but not a capability, for learning. Remember, learning how to learn and thinking about thinking are the two most effective interventions, regardless of ability.

Thinkspirational

If you find the idea of setting up a Metacognition Programme daunting, or would like a whole school INSET for your staff on the strategies outlined in this book, Thinkspirational can offer the following:

Staff INSET

Outlining many strategies (and more) included in this book, and tailored to your particular setting needs and demands. A school version of this book, bespoke to your requirements, can be produced and supplied.

Student Training

A whole day of workshops for students, covering the key skills you feel they need. This is a very practical and relevant experience for them all, and leads to a term of work.

Parent Workshop

A great deal of buy-in can be achieved for parents via a fun and active workshop, placed at the tail-end of a Staff INSET or Student Training day.

Curriculum design and consultation

Working with teachers and SLT, a Metacognition curriculum can be designed for your particular setting, complete with guidance on how to deliver sessions to your students.

Contact *Thinkspirational* via email on thinkspirational@gmail.com for availability and pricing.

Well? What did you think?

The most important question about this book is 'was it helpful for you?' We at Teacherly want to reward your efforts to feedback to us, so have developed a reward system for your next order through us.

Each of these efforts earns at least 10% off your next order:

10% off - if you write a 3+ review on Amazon

10% off - if you write a blogpost review

10% off - if you include a link to Teacherly

10% off - if you reference this book in a public talk

10% - if you gain a review in printed form

Simply send us a screenshot or other to hello@teacherly.cc and we'll send you your voucher back.

In addition, we are happy to supply this book free-of-charge as a prize at any TeachMet which features Metacognition or Self-regulation as a talk. If you can think of any other way to share this book, please do let us know, and we'll organise a reward as a thanks to you.

The Teacherly Team

Small print: Maximum order size - £100. Discount not available 30 days after purchase.

Printed in Great Britain
by Amazon

50215314R00131